WHAT WAR
TAUGHT ME
ABOUT PEACE

Other works by Robert Muller:

Most of All, They Taught Me Happiness

New Genesis, Shaping a Global Spirituality

A Planet of Hope

Sima, mon amour, a French novel

The Desire to Be Human, edited by Robert Muller and Leo Zonneveld, an international compendium in honour of Teilhard de Chardin

Decide to . . . .

About Robert Muller:

Global Spirituality, Planetary Consciousness in the Thought of Teilhard de Chardin and Robert Muller, Margaret McGurn

Robert Muller, Sopratutto Mi Insegnarono la Felicità, by Alessandro Carletti

Hacia el Planeta de Dios, Diálogos con Robert Muller, by Hilda Berger

The World Core Curriculum in the Robert Muller Elementary School, by Gloria Crook

WHAT WAR TAUGHT ME ABOUT PEACE

Robert Muller

DOUBLEDAY & COMPANY, INC.
GARDEN CITY, NEW YORK
1985

Library of Congress Cataloging in Publication Data

Muller, Robert, 1923–
  What war taught me about peace.

  1. Muller, Robert, 1923–   . I. Title.
CT3150.M84A39 1985   341.23'3'0924 [B]
Library of Congress Catalog Card Number: 85-1661
ISBN: 0-385-23187-3

Contents

I dedicate this book to the fortieth anniversary of the United Nations and to the first forty years of a new global age without a world war. May God inspire the leaders of nations to resolve their conflicts and allow all humanity to celebrate in the year 2000 a World Bimillennium Celebration of Life and our entry into the first millennium of peace, friendship and happiness for all.

Foreword

In *Most of All, They Taught Me Happiness,* I highlighted some of the events, experiences and people who taught me to believe in the wonderful benefits one can derive from a positive, optimistic attitude toward life and the world. I hold the view that our planet is a unique miracle in the universe. I believe that the humblest person on earth is a prodigy never to be repeated again in all eternity. I consider every day of our lives to be an incredible privilege for which we must be deeply thankful to God. I am convinced that life can be great and worthwhile even under the worst circumstances. I hold that life, that stupendous glimpse of consciousness into the universe, is sacrosanct and allows for no wars, no violence, no killings in the name of any group, institution, nation, ideology, system or individual. I believe that to live or not to live the life given to us by God is the basic question.

I was born and raised in a borderland torn politically and culturally between two countries; I have seen my hometown evacuated twice and I know what it is to be a refugee. I have seen my family split by two nations; I have known Nazi dictatorship and occupation; I have been in prison and in the French underground, and I have worked for all my adult life in the United Nations during one of the most mind-boggling periods of human history. It would require a second existence to record such a life, filled as it has been with so much learning, seeing, thinking, dreaming and action during one of the most astonishing epochs of all times. Amid my tasks and travels, I was able to find here and there an hour, at dawn, at home, in a train, in a plane, or in a meeting, to record and save from oblivion some of the facts, events and outstanding people I have known. The dream of writing some day the synthesis of my thoughts and hopes for humanity's future will probably remain unfulfilled, impeded as it is by the demands of my daily work.[1] But right after the completion of *Most of All, They Taught Me Happiness*, I still had so much to tell that the present volume naturally ensued. I was also encouraged to continue my writing by the numerous warm letters received from readers of my first book. Oh God, this blessing alone would justify my sky-high gratitude to You! Should only one person somewhere on this planet be touched by my stories, should only one more ounce of peace, love, compassion, understanding, justice and kindness be added to this earth as a result of them, I will have been royally recompensed!

I do not have any luminous answers to humanity's quandaries, but honestly and painstakingly I have observed life, people, the world and the functioning of the human mind and heart under all climates. Perhaps someone will be able to extract a bit of enlightenment from these stories and anecdotes. They are all I can contribute to the art of living and the search for human wisdom. Contemporary philosophers and thinkers, whose world views are generally pessimistic, had no influence on me. Life itself was my teacher, a hard but admirable one. It gave me endlessly more joys and astonishment than sorrows and disappointments. I have known good and evil, beauty and blemish, love and hatred, peace and war, happiness and pain, but the more I ad-

---

[1.] Nevertheless, in *New Genesis* I came close to doing that.

vanced in life, the more I have concluded that life itself is the greatest of all gifts.

Humanity and the world are the two pillars of our concern, the two perennial objects of our labors and cares. After a lifetime spent in our globe's first universal organization, I believe that the files for the future are now ready and that we can make this planet into a wonderful place for all humans to live in, peacefully, comfortably, justly, happily, gratefully and with endless love for God's stupendous Creation.

Deeply rooted in peace and in war, this book is one more stone to the building of a happier world, of a brighter future and of a greater understanding of the art and mystery of life. These stories are therefore a sequel to *Most of All, They Taught Me Happiness,* and a bridge to further volumes in which I hope to chant until my last breath the greatness and miracle of life on our beautiful planet in the fathomless universe.

1

A Bird's-eye View

I was born in 1923 in the Belgian province of Eupen and Malmédy, formerly a German territory. My parents were from Alsace-Lorraine, a French region which had also previously been German. My grandfather held five successive nationalities without leaving his village. My father served in the German army from 1917 to 1918, and in the French army in 1919 and 1940.

I was a child when my parents returned from Belgium to Alsace-Lorraine, where my father, a hat maker like my grandfather and great-grandfather, opened a hat shop in the town of Sarreguemines on the border with Germany.

When World War II broke out, our town was evacuated and I pursued my French high school studies as a refugee in the cities of Lyon and Metz. My father was mobilized in the French army.

In 1940, after the defeat of France, my family returned to Alsace-Lorraine, which was again annexed by Germany. I finished high school under German rule and began studies in economics at the University of Heidelberg.

After several attempts to cross the border to France in order to avoid serving in the German army, I finally succeeded and joined the French Resistance under the name of Louis Parizot and later Marco. In retaliation, my father was imprisoned by the Germans.

In 1945, at the end of the war, I resumed my studies and received a doctorate of law and economics from the

University of Strasbourg. My thesis was on the Saar Territory.

In 1947 I won a contest of the French Students' Association for the United Nations with an essay on world government which earned me an internship and later employment with the United Nations in 1948.

During my thirty-seven years of service with the United Nations, I held numerous positions, among which were those of Political Adviser to the UN troops in Cyprus, Associate Director of the UN Natural Resources Division, Director of the UN Budget and Director of the Secretary-General's Executive Office. I worked directly with three Secretaries-General of the UN.

In 1975, I was entrusted with the coordination of the thirty-two specialized agencies and world programs of the UN. In 1978, I was appointed Secretary of the Economic and Social Council, in 1982 Assistant Secretary-General for economic and social services, and in 1984 Assistant-Secretary General for the commemoration of the fortieth anniversary of the UN.

I have been happily married for thirty-two years to Margarita Gallo, a former Chilean UN interne and delegate to the United Nations, who continues to do volunteer work for the United Nations Women's Guild, of which she was for several years the president. We have four children and live in the charming village of Dobbs Ferry on the shores of the beautiful river Mahicannituck or Great Waters in Constant Motion, more recently called the Hudson River.

I am immensely proud and grateful to be a United Nations official and I pledge to God to continue to work for the peace and happiness of this planet for as long as I live.

2

Of Uniforms

We must work relentlessly for a united, disarmed and uniform-free human society.

When I was a child in my homeland of Alsace-Lorraine, I often drew pride from the fact that I was born in a foreign country. I remember how proudly at the beginning of each school year, when the teacher asked us for our date and place of birth, I answered loud and clear: "Born in Eupen-Malmédy, Belgium." The heads of my classmates turned in surprise and with a tinge of envy: I was the only pupil born abroad! Later, however, I became more dubious about my privileged place of birth. The Belgian province of Eupen-Malmédy, like Alsace-Lorraine, had been German prior to World War I. My grandfather had a hat factory in Lorraine which was a subsidiary of a firm located in the little village of Weismes in Eupen-Malmédy, where the Battle of the Bulge was to take place many years later. When my father moved there to perfect his training as a hat maker and I was born, Eupen-Malmédy had become Belgian, and Alsace-Lorraine French. My father used to tell me: "At the age of eighteen you will be able to opt for the Belgian nationality, since you were born there." But he was wrong: when I reached that age, in 1941, both Eupen-Malmédy and Alsace-Lorraine were German again!

My first puzzlement about the national phenomenon came from the military who, unlike today, were very visible in those times. Belgian troops often marched through our village and, together with other children, I ran and danced in front of them as was then the custom. Later, when we moved to Alsace-Lorraine, I ran and danced in front of French troops! I was told that they were "good" soldiers too, "Allied troops," but I was really at odds to understand why Belgian soldiers had ornamental tufts called "pompons" hanging from their berets, while French troops did not. Somehow these pompons symbolized in my little mind something which had to be of a military essence. Their absence from French uniforms was a real puzzle for me.

Soon I was to learn that there were not only "good" troops but also "bad" ones. I learned this from the picture album of my father. There was no TV or radio at that time. To save on gas and later electricity, the family gathered in the evening around the kitchen table under an adjustable lamp hanging from the ceiling. We read silently or played games or did things with our hands, while Mother was busy making preserves or knitting for the winter, always caring for her family in one way or another. The best moments were when my father told us stories which taught us to distinguish between good and evil and gave us a code of conduct for our lives. Sometimes—and it was always a very special moment—he took out the family's album and showed us photographs: pictures of my grandparents, of the young couple he formed with our mother, of us as babies, of the main events in the lives of our relatives, scenes from Belgium, pictures of picnics and of memorable excursions, snapshots of snow and sled parties, of our first Christmas tree, of toys and gifts. Here again we learned intensely about life, from birth to death, through happiness and sorrow. Each picture was an occasion for a long human anecdote. Especially exciting were his stories relating to war and to his life as a soldier. But this is where I encountered my national contradictions: the albums showed pictures of him once as a German soldier and then as a French soldier! Why was the same man wearing two different uniforms? How could that be? I knew these uniforms by heart, down to the last detail. The helmets were different: the German was heavy, brutal, fierce-looking; the French was light, elegant, almost lovely. The German beret was flat, gray and dull; the French *beret de police* was graceful, blue like the sky, almost human. As a German soldier, my father looked stern and aggressive; as a French soldier, he was gentle and smiling. When I asked him why he wore two uniforms, he simply shrugged his shoulders and said:

"When I was seventeen, the Germans were our masters. They put me into their uniform and sent me to Schwerin, a city in the north of Germany; when the French came, they put me into their uniform and sent me to a French city called Toul. Do not ask me why. It is our fate in Alsace-Lorraine to be tossed from one side to another and to be forced to shoot in opposite directions even on friends and family members!"

My puzzlement became even greater when I heard references to some strange and forgotten foreign troops who had roamed about our region a long time ago. When I came home very dirty and with my clothes torn, my mother used to say: *"Oh! Du loosh wie a Schlowak!"* (You look like a Slovak!) Who were those Slovaks? I learned that they were members of a certain Wallenstein army which ransacked and burned our villages during the Thirty Years War. Their memory was still entrenched in the folk tradition. Similarly, when I was very naughty, my father sometimes threatened me that *"De Schwede wäre Disch frässe."* (The Swedes will devour you.) This was a reference to Swedish troops who had no less fiercely ransacked our region during that same war.[1] These stories impressed me very much. Everything I saw around me, despite my family's poverty, was so beautiful: nature, the birds, the flowers, trees, animals, the fields, autumn leaves, snow, the sky, a fire in the hearth, people. But what were those uniforms, those arms and horror stories doing in such a magnificent world? I just could not understand it, and I still cannot understand it today.

At my grandfather's home, in the village of Sarralbe, I heard more war stories. In front of the hat factory there was a very large courtyard, several acres wide, along the Saar River. I loved every part of it, above all the sections reserved for domestic animals: the chicken coops, the rabbits' cages, the pig stalls and the sheeps' quarters. No food refuse was thrown away in those days: potato and vegetable peelings, damaged greens, food remnants from the table were all preciously kept and cooked with bran to provide a liquid brew called "Suff," which was taken in a pail to the pigs. My grandfather used to tell me that during World War I, a large part of the courtyard was occupied by a prisoners' camp for English soldiers captured by the Germans:

"There were barbed wires and barracks all over the place. The prisoners received very little food and many of them died of tuberculosis and deprivation. It was a dreadful sight to see these poor devils from our house. To reach the pig stalls, one had to walk along the barbed fence and each time your aunt Eulalie was taking the "Suff" to the pigs, the poor prisoners were stretching their hands through the wire, begging for the repulsive brew."

Aunt Eulalie fell in love with one of the English prison-

---

[1] Religious hatred animated the Swedish troops. Their flag showed Lorraine as a woman cut in half from head to bottom, flanked by soldiers torturing her with swords and torches. Lorraine was struck by famine, pest and an invasion of wolves. There were many cases of anthropophagy. This happened a little more than three hundred years ago.

ers. After the war he returned to Sarralbe to court her. While he stayed at my grandfather's house, he used to rise early in the morning to take a swim in the Saar. One morning he did not come back. The family waited in vain for him. Men searched the river with long wooden poles and found his drowned body. He was the only son of an English couple. My aunt Eulalie later married the local schoolteacher, but in our family the memory of the young Englishman was always kept, and bonds of friendship were maintained with his family in England.

I still had not seen any "bad" soldiers. Although we lived in full view of Germany, there were no German troops on the other side of the border. The Versailles treaty did not allow Germany to have any troops. Moreover, the Saar[2] Territory was a special region placed under international administration. In the streets of its capital, Saarbrücken, one could see officers from several countries, the first international peace-keeping force ever.

But this did not last very long and all kinds of strange uniforms began to appear in our region. In 1935, the Saar Territory voted for its return to Germany, and soon thereafter most Saarländers were wearing Nazi uniforms: children, girls, boys, men and women. I still remember a picture which appeared in a French magazine. It showed a dozen boots of various sizes standing in front of a door, with the caption: "A German family"! Only the disabled and old people were not allowed to wear uniforms. Hitler considered them a disgrace and as belonging in tombs. They could not serve his power dreams and were useless, harmful consumers of resources. We discovered after the war that there

---

[2] The same river and the same piece of land are spelled Saar in German and Sarre in French. The spelling of the name Muller changes to Müller when the Germans are in command.

was a clinic in Strasbourg where Nazi doctors systematically put an end to the lives of handicapped and old people. My heart rejoices today, while Hitler would turn in his tomb if he knew, that the United Nations was holding an international year for the 450 million disabled persons of this planet and a world conference for the elderly. . . . The deluge of Nazi uniforms—black ones, brown ones, green ones—was accompanied by a flood of flags, banners, and military bands. There were incessant parades. It seemed as if Lucifer and his bodyguards had emerged from the earth and had invaded Germany. Our house was located on a hill. From my window I could see Germany and it gave me a strange, eerie feeling to contemplate a "foreign" country. I could see glimmers of torches and hear drums late into the night. Our region sounded sometimes like an African jungle on the warpath.

On the French side too the face of the earth was changing. A huge underground fortress, the Maginot Line, was being built all along the border. At our latitude, the fortress had to be interrupted, for the subsoil was an unstable sandy mass from which salt had been extracted since the Romans, lately by injecting hot water into the earth. No underground fortress could be built in such terrain. This break in the line was filled with troops and artificial lakes. All kinds of strange soldiers appeared: Africans, Muslims, Malgaches, Indochinese, people from the various French colonies. Nazi newspapers published pictures of them with racist captions which I had better spare the reader. The courtyard of my grandfather was once again requisitioned and occupied by soldiers and barracks. Where twenty years ago English prisoners had suffered from hunger and cold, Africans and Asians were now shivering. Many of them died of tuberculosis in our wet and sunless climate. I liked these new troops very much: they had exotic uniforms and ways of life; they spread little carpets in front of them and prayed to their

God, facing the sky in the direction of a city called Mecca; they cooked strange, fragrant, spicy foods and sometimes roasted entire muttons on spits in the open air. A wonderful sergeant named Bou Sidi became my friend. He told me exciting stories about his people and sometimes performed dances of his tribe for the villagers. Behind the different uniforms, races and faces, there were the same human hearts and dreams. On each breast, in each pocketbook, there were pictures of a wife, children, a fiancée, parents, brothers and sisters. But the uniforms were different on both sides of the border, and deadly arms were aimed at each other. Something dreadful was in preparation. The air of Alsace-Lorraine was once again filled with menace.

How did my family react to these symptoms? My father was the most outspoken. He profoundly disliked the Germans and their discipline, and preferred the French and their staunch sense of freedom. I will never forget this remark he once made to me:

"Son, if the Germans ever come back to this region with all their order, discipline, obedience and efficiency, I will pack my pajamas and toothbrush in a little suitcase and leave immediately for France."

As for my mother, she deeply distrusted all political groupings, especially nations, which she considered to be in the end detrimental to the individual. Only one social group counted for her in the world: the family. She would have sacrificed any party, institution, politician, flag, hero, ideology, religion or nation to her kin. She used to say that if the world were about to perish, human beings would only care for their own family. This deeply entrenched belief of hers has left an indelible mark on me: having been prevented by her from even joining the Boy Scouts, I have generally kept away during my life from any associations, clubs, movements and political parties. And God knows how many have been offered to me, all promising in one form or another the heavens and happiness! If at times I succumbed to the temptation, it was not for long. My self, my family, humanity and God were the only entities I ever recognized, served and was ready to defend. When I left for the United Nations in 1948, my mother took my hands, looked deeply into my eyes and said:

"Son, now you are going to work for the only other family worth caring for in this world: the human family. Never forget it and never work for any one country." I obeyed her faithfully.

As for my grandfather, he was born a Frenchman in 1867, became German in 1871, French again in 1918, German in 1940 and French again in 1945, practically without leaving his village! His attitude was yet a different one: he was always critical of those who were present and sympathetic to those who had left! When the French were in Alsace-Lorraine he yearned for German order. When the Germans were there he dreamed of French freedom! He used to point in two different directions of the road when he spoke about the one or the other!

Today, so many years later, as I write these lines, I find in my own family all the major social contradictions I was to encounter in the United Nations. Who was right? My grandfather, the opportunist? My father, the freedom lover? Or my mother, the life-giver and humanist? I believe she was right. She was closest to the truth. She could not be fooled by anyone, and someday the world will look as she wanted it to look: a world of families lived by individuals for individuals, a vast family of families.

I must cite here another type of uniform which came to the fore in 1936 and perplexed me a lot: the Nazi fashion of wearing uniforms and making people march in the streets with banners and fanfare had contaminated Europe far beyond the borders of Germany. In France, a new political party or movement sprang up, the "blue-shirts" of a certain Colonel Laroque. Its members were very visible in the streets of our town. There were hundreds of them, especially young people, all hoping that Colonel Laroque would become the French Hitler. Their local chief was a miller from a neighboring village, a Mr. Goepff, whose daughter Monique, a very nice girl who totally disagreed with her father, was a classmate of mine. The militants marched through the streets of our town every Sunday morning, dressed in sky-blue shirts crossed diagonally with shining leather straps, wearing black Canadian mounties' pants and black boots, aping awkwardly the German goosestep march, while the Nazis were parading in the same fashion on the other side of the river! There was no way of getting bored in my hometown in those times! Since the miller also had a bread-delivery service, which earned him a lot of money, and was engaged in all sorts of business ventures, the people did not take his politics very seriously. He was basically an opportunist, and the main purpose of the movement was to frighten people about the Communists and the Jews.

As I look back on those times, I cannot help noticing that it was always the same people who wore uniforms. I just cannot visualize some of our neighbors other than clad in uniforms: their blue-shirt outfit was later replaced by the brown Nazi uniform. There seems to be always in every country and human group a certain percentage of people who need public exhibition and who will join any movement that offers them a uniform. They are despised and hated by the rest of the population. They usually know it and retaliate when they are in power. They must have had some basic frustration in life and can take the most awful revenge. They are ready to serve any dictatorship or extreme regime, left or right. I hope sociologists will someday seriously study this most troublesome political species.

In 1938 our hometown was evacuated the first time under the threat of war over Czechoslovakia. We took refuge in the French Jura mountains. I was then fifteen years old and the question of our own uniforms would soon arise for me and for my cousins. What were my feelings toward these menacing events? Like my father, I was deeply fond of France's humanism and sense of liberty, but I also liked Germany's writers, romanticism and great musicians. What I hated were the uniforms and the faces of those who wore them. During the year of the exhibition of the Lord's Holy Robe in Trier, I was arrested for having played the "Marseillaise" on my harmonica while Nazi troops were parading provokingly in front of the pilgrims. But the real tests regarding my likes and dislikes were still to come, and I would be given ample opportunities to observe the contradictions of good and bad in human nature and in the political fabric of our planet.

Later I was to wear a uniform myself. It was a very shabby and incomplete uniform. But it was all we had in the French underground: khaki pants, a khaki shirt, a belt, an armband, a Colt revolver and a Sten submachinegun. I never made it to a jacket and headgear. Today I trust that it was God's will that I should never wear a full uniform.

There is one tiny place on earth which epitomizes this period of my life and where I love to wander alone with my thoughts and memories whenever I return to Alsace-Lorraine. It is the cemetery of Sarralbe, located on a hill called the Hill of the Huns, in a vast plain known as the Plain of the Huns. In that valley and on that hill, the Huns dwelled when they invaded the region. They were stopped a few miles away by a Roman fortress built by Julius Caesar, which gave the next village its name: Kaeskastel (Caesaris castellum). It was murmured in my family that we were of Hun descent, and there was little doubt about it in my mind when I looked at the features of my grandfather and of my aunt Eulalie. On the Hill of the Huns there is a wild, forsaken area called the Galgenberg, where the gallows stood in ancient times. Today it is reserved for the burial of those who commit suicide. In the regular cemetery my grandparents rest in peace. In another section are the tombs of the English prisoners who died in my grandfather's courtyard during World War I. In still another part lie buried African, French, Russian and Yugoslav soldiers of World War II. My last visit always takes me to the tomb of a young man from my hometown. He had been executed after the war for having collaborated with the Nazis and denounced several young Alsace-Lorrainers who had escaped from the German army. He had paid me two visits in France, bringing me news from my family and asking me to organize a resistance group with other compatriots. He pretended to be working for the Allies and even showed me an American passport, which allowed him to go to London. It is almost certain that the Germans' attempt to arrest me (See "Thank You, Dr. Coué," in *Most of All, They Taught Me Happiness)* was due to him. Before his execution he was allowed to marry a girl whom I knew. From that union in prison a child was born who never saw her father. It is that tomb, the image of the skeleton in it and of the bullets in the skeleton which give me the last shudder when I visit the Hill of the Huns. What a waste it had all been! Romans, Huns, Swedes, Slovaks, French, Germans, British, Africans, Russians, Yugoslavs, Americans. What did all these labels mean, attached basically to the same human flesh? Why had these men had to die; why had their families, their mothers, their children had to suffer as a consequence of these names? What a sight it would be if all these dead soldiers were resurrected on the

Hill of the Huns,[3] in their checkered uniforms, pointing at their wounds and asking with despair: "Why? Why? Why? Why am I here? Why did I die? Why am I far from my family? What good was it for? Where are the leaders, where is the nation, where is the cause I was killed for? Why was my adult life aborted?"

Yes, what a waste it had been! How could the ambitions of men be so contrary to the greatness of life and to the beauty of our planet! All these deaths and sufferings had been utterly in vain. The world would never be at peace as long as it was divided into power-drunk, lustful and sovereign nations, as long as it was not *one world* and *one human family*. My youth had prepared me well for service with the United Nations!

And yet, today, when my thoughts wander back to those times, it gives me immense comfort to think that this region of the planet is now at peace. No new war has swept over the tomb of my grandfather. He would have never dared to dream of the peace we enjoy today! If such a miracle was possible between France and Germany, surely it will also be possible between all nations of the globe. Europe has learned its lessons well. There are today a European Common Market, a Council of Europe, a European Parliament, a European Court of Human Rights. And when a problem arises between France and Germany, the Presidents of the two countries pick up the phone and talk it over. There is no longer any question of preferring division to cooperation and hatred to understanding. I remember that when I accompanied Secretary-General Waldheim on a visit to the President of Italy, I heard the latter comment: "If anyone would advise us West Europeans to return to the

---

[3.] I dream sometimes that a film may be made someday, bringing back to life these soldiers and showing all the wars and battles which took place on this little piece of earth.

prewar system of suspicion, subversion, alliances and divisions, we would ask him to get his head examined!" The example of France and Germany must be followed by other nations, especially by the U.S. and the U.S.S.R. This wisdom must now spread to the entire world. We must never give up hope, but believe in the progress of the human race and work very hard for it. Yes, we must follow Europe's example and create the spirit and institutions of a United World.

In my office at the United Nations today are displayed two military symbols of my life: a German helmet from World War II pierced by bombshells, and a sky-blue helmet of the UN peace-keeping forces. The first represents a past which should be eradicated once and for all like a pest from this planet. The second should be acceptable as a transition to a totally unarmed and uniform-free world.

As I finished writing this story I went to peruse the illustrations of my grandfather's German encyclopedia from the year 1894. They show hundreds of uniforms from the European armies of that time. Today, most of these nations are gone, and all these uniforms have vanished into museums. May God help us soon to put all remaining military uniforms of this planet where they really belong: museums.

3

A Boy's Letter
to a Prime Minister

Never fail to denounce an injustice to the person at the top.

September 1939. I was sitting in my room, reading romantic literature, my soul filled with happiness and poetry about the beauty of the world.

From my window I glanced over the Saar River into Germany. During the last few years the woods had disappeared from the hills on the German side and had been replaced by wheat fields and a new village—Adolf Hitler Dorf. Its inhabitants were metallurgical workers who also did some farming and small animal husbandry in order to increase the self-sufficiency of the German Reich. Along the river and its tributary, the Blies, humans once again were divided by hatred. There were constant incidents. The Germans organized innumerable noisy parades along the river, appealing to the beastly side of human nature. On the French side, we did not remain passive either: we sang the "Marseillaise" at the opening of each soccer game in the stadium which was located right along the border. The Nazis retaliated by holding political meetings opposite the stadium at the exact time of the opening of the games in order to drown the sounds of the French national anthem under their Teutonic marches. Hatred was escalating again along a peaceful river and under the same sun, arousing the emotions of the people like a vicious tide. Noise, colors, words, music, uniforms, sport, day and night, the living and the dead, everything was mobilized to bolster the "greatness" of each nation.

But this was for me the beautiful age of sixteen, when to be alive and to approach adulthood and love were tantamount to paradise. The writings of Lamartine, Chateaubriand, Goethe and Schiller transported me to heaven. The preceding year our town had been evacuated a first time. We had fled to the French Jura mountains, to the summer house of former tenants who had moved away from the border when they saw the turn of events. Our place of refuge was not far from the region where Lamartine had lived. I had walked in his woods, reading his poetry with ecstasy, considering him the greatest literary genius the earth had ever borne.

I was sharing my thoughts and feelings with my beloved authors when my mother climbed the staircase, entered my room and said:

"Boy, come down and help us pack. War is going to break out at any moment. Our town is again being evacuated. Our car has already been requisitioned, but the driver can still take us to our place of refuge with a load of clothes and food if we can leave early enough. Every minute counts. Get ready and pack your things."

I answered:

"I could not care less about that war. I hate all wars. Why should anyone, especially a madman like Hitler, have the right to interrupt the course of my life and of my studies?"

My mother looked at me sternly. Her blue eyes turned into cold steel and became filled with a world of hard messages and thoughts. Then, without a comment, she slapped me in the face with a strength that almost knocked me senseless.

She left the room without a word. I had gotten her message; I packed my clothes and went downstairs to help with the preparations of the rest of the family.

Many years later, when addressing a group of veterans visiting the United Nations in New York, a French officer, upon hearing that I came from the town of Sarreguemines, had this comment:

"You must have left your town hurriedly, for when we entered it, we still found dishes with food and unfinished meals on the tables." This comment, indeed, describes better than anything else what our evacuation was like.

In the afternoon the driver who had taken possession of our car drove us to Lutzelbourg, a little locality forty miles away from the border, where my mother had rented in anticipation of these events a small apartment usually only occupied during the summer by vacationers. Days ago my father had been mobilized into the French army and had left for a destination unknown to us in a vast underground fortress called the Maginot Line.

After leaving us at our place of refuge, the driver and the car returned to Sarreguemines and we never saw them again.[1] The following day, war was declared, annihilating my lofty, romantic dreams and placing me at the age of sixteen at the helm of the family. My mother tried to live on her meager savings, which were rapidly dwindling under the effects of inflation. The rent for our apartment was high and the priest who owned it wanted us to get rid of our dog. So we moved to a cheaper abode, an attic in a farmhouse of a hamlet called Trois-Maisons (Three Houses). It was a tiny and poor hamlet indeed, located on a desolate plateau near

---

[1] After the war we learned that Jules Frank, the driver, had died in a German concentration camp.

Phalsbourg, above Lutzelbourg, swept by cold and rainy winds, a region deeply marked by wars and desolation. We could walk both to Lutzelbourg and to Phalsbourg, two places for which my heart soon developed a deep affection: Lutzelbourg for its red sandstones, its hills and little valleys densely covered with pine trees, its crystal-clear river, and also a young Parisian girl who was staying at one of the patrician houses and whom I loved madly, without ever daring to address a single word to her; Phalsbourg for its history, its fortifications half sunk back into nature, its majestic church, its description by Goethe, the fact that it was the birthplace of two famous Alsatian authors, Erckmann and Chatrian,[2] and the starting point of a memorable journey described in a wonderful French schoolbook: *A Tour of France by Two Children*. How often at the United Nations was I tempted to write a similar book entitled *A Tour of the World by Two Children!*

Although war had been declared, there was little military activity at the front. The Germans did not attack France until May of the following year. For the moment, the daily communiqués were all alike:

"Some shooting and patrol activity on both sides of the Blies and the Saar Rivers."

Our evacuated town was apparently quite tranquil, and soon we heard reports that some of the rich merchants were able to enter the city with trucks and evacuate their merchandise. The refugees who lived in the region were very bitter about this. One of the main topics of conversation among the refugees was how to get hold of a winter coat. With the onset of the war this merchandise had disappeared from the stores. We too wished to go home and bring

[2.] Little could I dream that forty-five years later, in 1984, I would stand in front of their monument in Phalsbourg, holding in my hands the Erckmann-Chatrian Prize received for my novel *Sima, mon amour!*

back more of our belongings, but we were not given any permits. I became deeply infuriated with this injustice when I saw trucks carrying merchandise from our home-town drive through the streets of Phalsbourg toward safer places. I talked with the drivers and indeed they were evac-uating the merchandise from the stores of the rich mer-chants. I sat down and wrote a letter to Mr. Daladier, the Prime Minister of France, describing the conditions of the refugees on the eve of winter and the privileged treatment being given to the rich, who, as usual, had the right connec-tions. I did not mince my words and I found it prudent not to show my letter to my mother before mailing it.

In the meantime she had convinced a French officer to give her and a friend a pass to a place called Rohrbach, where the husband of the latter was serving in the Maginot Line. The two women hired a taxi and a driver, pulled down the curtains inside the car—at that time automobiles had elegant interior curtains and even little vases for flowers—and we traveled happily through the combat zone to the Maginot Line, where the husband of my mother's friend was called out of the underground fortress and had a joyous reunion with his wife. The soldiers were all from Alsace-Lorraine. They offered us a mighty fine meal, and I listened attentively to their conversations carried out in our dialect. Thus I became aware of another injustice:

They were bitterly complaining that there were so few "Frenchmen" on the front. Most troops consisted of Alsace-Lorrainers and colonial regiments. Only the officers were "French." My compatriots did not hide their intention not to fight under such circumstances if the Germans attacked. They had no illusions either regarding the outcome. One of them who had served as a German officer in World War I was telling us that when he joined his French regiment he was ordered to guard a bridge with a stick because there were no weapons! These facts as well as the disastrous defeat of France a year later never left my mind. Whenever I hear someone laud the superiority of the French intelligentsia, I cannot help remember how some of these brainy geniuses had mismanaged the country, letting it be crushed within a few weeks by a ridiculous, uneducated little corporal-painter called Adolf Hitler. The Maginot Line itself, the costly brainchild of such a genius, proved to be totally useless: Hitler's planes overflew it and his tanks and infantry invaded France via Belgium.

My mother wanted to press her luck and go to our hometown, located right on the border. We reached the entrance of the city, but at a checkpoint a French officer looked into our car and when he saw two women and a boy circulating freely in the combat zone, he blew his top and had us expelled by the shortest route under military escort. Despite this unsuccessful ending, we had greatly enjoyed our trip and the two women were very proud of their exploit.

A few days later, knocks at our poor little attic door woke us up late in the evening. My mother opened the door and we saw two gendarmes from Phalsbourg, who asked whether a certain Robert Muller lived there. I reviewed rapidly in my mind whether I had committed any mischief, but I could not remember any. My mother offered chairs to the two men. One of them extracted from a leather bag a bundle of papers on top of which I saw my letter to the Prime Minister! It was underlined in red in several places and annotated in the margin. The gendarme said to my mother:

"Your son's letter has been read and commented on by the Prime Minister himself. He has asked the proper department to investigate his accusations and these papers are all reports prepared in response to his request. Apparently your son has won his case. We have been instructed to issue passes to you and to all the refugees in the region. You will be able to go home and bring back your possessions. Please come to our office tomorrow morning. We will put a small truck and a driver at your disposal. Here is your *laissez-passer.*"

I had remained mouse-still during the entire conversation. Nevertheless, when the two gendarmes left, they threw me a nasty look which I interpreted as a mixture of hatred and admiration for a rotten kid who had had the guts to write directly to the Prime Minister!

My mother did not allow me this time to accompany her, but when she returned from our hometown with a truckload of clothes, linen, blankets and preserves, she had a wonderful and thoughtful gift for me: in a large box she had rescued and brought for me the seventeen volumes of my beloved German encyclopedia, which my grandfather had given to me: an 1894 edition of the Meyers Konversations-Lexikon. It remained one of the few memorabilia from my youth, because when we returned home in 1940, our house had been completely plundered. Later, in America, I would show its beautiful illustrations to my sons, as my father and grandfather had shown them to me.

I have drawn two important lessons from this anecdote:

First—if you see an injustice, do not wait for a better world; denounce it right away to the person at the top, even if you have little chance of being heard; you will at least feel better and sometimes you might even get results.

Secondly—when I became myself a close collaborator of three Secretaries-General of the UN, I made it a point to ensure that worthy letters written by humble, well-intentioned people were always seen by them, acted upon and answered. The right to complain and to receive a reply should be made a basic human right, for government is here for the people and not for the tranquillity of the bureaucrats.

Later I learned that President John Kennedy set the

rule that every hundredth letter from the vast amount of mail a President receives every day from citizens be handed to him unopened, so that he could read it and keep in touch with his people. This good practice should be made a rule for the heads of state of all countries of the world. It would break the barriers which their entourage usually builds around them under the pretext of protecting their time.

4

Of Good Teachers I

A good teacher is one who arouses the enthusiasm of students for life and learning.

At one or another time, all human beings look back, think of their teachers and remember with particular fondness those who exercised a profound and sometimes decisive influence. After a life full of events and learning, my thoughts frequently turn to my teachers. And I am astonished to find how many educators a human being can have nowadays in a rich country. A cursory count of mine indicates that I had nearly one hundred! Sadly enough, I cannot even remember the names of most of them. Two, however, left a lasting impression on me. Those could have been teachers of princes and kings, and I owe them a great debt of gratitude.

One was an assistant professor at our high school in Sarreguemines. His name was Hehn. He came from the same village as my mother, who held him in high esteem. He never made it to full professor because World War I had prevented him from finishing his studies. He was the librarian of our lycée and was allowed once in a while to substitute as a teacher of German. Until I knew him, my studies had been good but dull. My enthusiasms were elsewhere: they were with the people and life in the streets, with cherry trees and birds, with brooks and meadows, with the four seasons, with gardening, with a farm, with my father's

hat making shop. School did not contain life, it did not really
deal with life until Mr. Hehn came along. As if he knew that
he had only a few short weeks to leave a mark on us, he
worked fast and intensively. From the first day, he kept us
spellbound despite his strict discipline. Life soon entered
our classroom with its people, the cherry trees, the streets,
the seasons, the meadows, the dreams and the loves of each
of us, from cars and airplanes to music and art. He put his
finger right on the heart of each student. He reduced the
academic purpose of the course to what it really was,
namely the learning of a mere technique: the German language. But behind that language, as behind all five thousand
languages of this planet, are a human being's life and aspira-
tions, dreams, songs and endeavors, outreaching for the
stars, humanity's wonderful diversity and passion for beauty
and good in all its forms. His tools were Goethe and Schiller,
a painting, a poem, an old clock, a legend, the etymology of
a word, the Lord's Prayer in old high-Germanic or an article
in the newspaper of the day. Through these instruments he
told us about life, he taught us life. In order to gain rapid
access to its riches, vocabulary and grammar had to be
mastered quickly. The sooner we could forget about them,
the better it was, for we were to deal with the essentials of
life. For the first time, I read German with pleasure. I had
an alarm clock next to me at home to see how much and fast
I could read in that language. From then on, I knew the
secret: education, sciences and humanities are only techniques. Behind them are the sky, life, the search and discovery of oneself, the forces that hold everything together in
heaven and on earth. Passion, enthusiasm, deep belief in
oneself, love for life, obsession with life, these are the great
motors of learning and human happiness. I became a joyful
student and managed, through successive enthusiasms and
curiosity for various subjects, to master the essential techniques and branches of knowledge. I knew that they were

only a means of "zeroing in" on life. From then on, my teachers barely understood me and simply classified me as an "exceptional" student. I progressively became unbeatable in any subject, except when I crossed the path of students who had made that field their passion. Today I find these classmates to be top authorities in their professions, in France, in Europe and sometimes in the world.

In 1939, when the war broke out and we became refugees, my mother wanted me to continue my high school studies in a school far away from the front. So she sent me to the city of Lyon where I stayed with former tenants of ours and was lucky enough to go to one of the most prestigious French secondary schools: the Lycée Ampère. Coming from a small provincial town, I felt like a dumb peasant among students who had been trained for years by some of the best teachers of France. God, how good they were! But only one of them could match Mr. Hehn. Truly, he was another Hehn, except that he was on top of the academic ladder and one of the most admired and honored professors in the country. He had graduated from the famous École Normale Supérieure in Paris, was a doctor of letters and had even passed the reputed entrance competition for the Comédie Française. He was our teacher of humanities—French literature and Latin—and thus our main instructor. Our grade was the all-important *classe de première* at the end of which a crucial examination, the first baccalaureate, paved the way to university.

I stayed in Lyon for only three months, but this brief period of time changed my life. Why?

Well, because, above all, Professor Cumin was giving us the example of a great, happy, life-impassioned man who would not have traded his profession for that of President of France, as he once told us. He loved to teach and to mold young people into solid, balanced, happy human beings. He loved to be with us. He loved to live his life all over again for

us. He loved to share everything he knew. He played for us
the tragedies and comedies of life, sometimes to the point of
exclaiming "Let's not have any recess," to which we agreed
enthusiastically. He had invariably his own original
thoughts about everything and was totally unimpressed by
the views of academic authorities. There was nothing he
abhorred more than a student who was repeating the opinions of someone else. I will never forget how he treated me
when I arrived. Our class was very large: it consisted of
more than fifty students. Being accustomed to smaller
classes in a provincial town, I thought that I could remain
pretty anonymous in such a crowd. But I did not go unnoticed for long, and on one of the first days, Professor Cumin
abruptly asked me this question:

"Muller, what is the central theme of Corneille's drama
Le Cid?"

Caught off guard in my tranquillity, I answered hastily
what I had read in the textbooks: "It is the struggle between
love and duty."

The whole class turned silent as if something momentous was about to happen. Professor Cumin's long, inspired
face became even longer and totally aghast. The upper part
of his body sagged on his desk, as if thunder had struck him.
He closed his eyes and actually managed to look several
years older. His body progressively glided down behind his
desk until he disappeared. Then the whole class, unable to
hold it any longer, broke out into an indescribable pandemonium of laughter!

I looked around, incredulous at having unleashed such
a scene. When the noise had abated, Professor Cumin
emerged from behind his desk, pointed his long artistic
finger at me, swallowed his first aborted attempt to speak
and finally, with his hands, imitated the movements of a
boat floating on the sea. Having found his voice again, he
uttered these words:

"Petit bateau."[1] (Little boat.)

He then spoke to me sternly:

"I hope sincerely never to hear again such sottishness in this class. I wanted *your* opinion and not that of a textbook. Make it a sacred rule in your life to be always yourself, to know yourself and to rely only upon yourself. Be a man. Master your brain and heart and remain unimpressed by anyone else in this world. Accept an idea to be the truth only if *you* are convinced of it."[2]

And then, from his serious inspired face came this order:

"Recite the principles of thinking by Descartes."

I knew their content but I was unable to repeat the exact words.

He commented:

"A few moments ago I gave you rule Number One for life. Now I give you rule Number Two: never forget, under any circumstances, the principles of thought by Descartes. Know them by heart. Recite them in the morning, before or after prayer, as you wish, but recite them every day of your life. You can forget everything I am teaching you, you can forget me, but never forget the principles of Descartes. They will help you out in any situation. They must be your brain's bible."

How could any of his students ever forget them! He

---

[1] From a popular French children's song in which a little girl asks her mother if boats have legs. And the mother answers: "Of course, little stupid one, otherwise how could they walk on the water?" Professor Cumin meant that my answer was about as dumb.

[2] I followed this principle all my life. It earned me in 1983 the Integrity Prize of the John Roger Foundation, an award based on the same principles of truth and personal integrity developed by Descartes and Buckminster Fuller.

often interrupted his French or Latin classes and snapped this question at us:

"Dupont. Les principes de Descartes. Vite." (Dupont, recite the principles of Descartes, quick.)

How right he was and how grateful I have been to him for his unforgettable lessons. I never ceased to heed his admonitions. In learning about life, in my work at the UN, in preparing a compromise, a proposal or a plan of action, I often remembered his words:

"Think for yourself. Do not accept the opinions of others blindly. Get to the root of a problem, and think, think, think . . ."

As for the principles of Descartes, I do not have to recite them any more, for they have become part of the most intimate functioning of my mind, as they have for most French people. Here they are:

Considering that logic is composed of such a multitude of precepts, I thought that the following four rules would suffice for me, provided I took the firm and unfailing resolution always to observe them:

The first is never to accept anything to be the truth unless I know it clearly to be so, i.e., to avoid carefully any precipitation and preconception, and to include in my judgments only that which would present itself so clearly and so forcefully to my mind as to leave no room whatever for any doubt.

The second is to divide each difficulty into as many parts as is feasible and necessary to resolve it.

The third is to conduct my thoughts in an orderly fashion, beginning with the simplest and most identifiable objects, so as to increase by degrees my knowledge of the most composite ones, and assuming some order even between those which do not follow each other naturally.

And the last is to resort in all cases to such complete

enumerations and such general reviews as to exclude any possibility of omission.

I have been led to add two further personal rules to these principles:

"Always think in terms of the entire planet, for everything is interdependent in this world."

"Always think far into the future, for the seeds of tomorrow are being planted today."

I owe another piece of good advice to Professor Cumin.

One day I approached him after class with this question:

"I like your counsel regarding self-reliance and originality. I find no difficulty either in applying Descartes' rules of thinking. But one obstacle seems to me insurmountable: I cannot overcome the poverty of my style. As you know, in Alsace-Lorraine we are part of two cultures and we use two languages. As a result we are perfect in neither of them. Since German is a highly flexible idiom, we can hold our own in it, but with French it is a different story: our teachers tell us quite bluntly that we will never be able to write like French writers. Perfect and beautiful French is apparently beyond our reach."

He looked at me gently with his warm, intelligent face, put his arm around my shoulders and said:

"Man, do not listen to such rubbish. You can perfectly acquire any style you wish in any language. Style is only a technique subordinate to thought and feeling. There is nothing easier than to learn a style. Follow my advice: select a famous author whom you like particularly, for example, Voltaire, or better Sainte-Beuve since you will have to write literary essays at your exams. Copy each day ten lines from his works in a notebook. Copy them slowly for no less than ten minutes so as to learn them almost by heart. Do this for at least six months. From time to time, read the entire text you have copied. Mark my words: in six months you will write exactly like Voltaire or Sainte-Beuve. The same holds true for any other style. It is as simple as that."

I followed his advice and his prediction came true: I found myself one day writing exactly the same long, complex sentences of Sainte-Beuve, having acquired his rhythm and structure of expression. Writing became from then on a joy. My thoughts, feelings and ideas came with extreme ease, all wrapped up in good words and sentences. I later used the same technique for German in university and English and Spanish at the United Nations. Whenever I have much writing to do, I turn to my notebooks and read what I have copied years ago. And there it comes: I write again like the authors I had selected.

Professor Cumin was right. Words, sentences, languages and the mechanisms of thinking are only techniques and tools for the discovery and expression of the deeper functioning and meaning of life. They should never be allowed to be obstacles to the full flowering of one's abilities. Given too much importance, as is so often the case, they can inhibit a person from becoming a full and happy being by shutting off the interplay between inborn mental, sentimental and creative forces and the surrounding world. Some writers and professors erect style as a "rare gift," difficult to acquire by common mortals. They thus seek to establish a monopoly and superiority over others. In reality there is no such inborn gift. No baby is born talking like Shakespeare. I would not be surprised if all writers did not follow a technique similar to that of Professor Cumin. Only a few authors, though, have had the courage to admit it. For example, Benjamin Franklin writes in his autobiography that he memorized sentences by famous authors and a few days later tried to formulate the same thought in his own words. He then compared the result with the original model.

When spring 1940 came, I was recalled to Lorraine, for

my mother had found a place to live in Metz where I could go to the local school and stay with her and my sister. I was happy to return closer to home, but I had a broken heart over leaving Professor Cumin. He had taught me so much in so little time, for the above are only a few of the unforgettable teachings he instilled in me. Professor Cumin is the only teacher to whom I have ever written a letter saying that I would never forget him as long as I lived and that I felt like crying because I had to leave him. He sent me a warm, encouraging reply, which ended with these words: *"Oubliez-moi."* (Forget me.) *"Gnôthi seauthon."*[3] (Know yourself.)

And today, after so many years, I wonder what my life would have been if I had not been a refugee and if I had missed the extraordinary opportunity of Professor Cumin's teachings, which truly changed my life.

For sure, I would not have become a writer. I would not have dared. Moreover, he taught me to be strong, to have confidence and optimism at a time when I was living far away from my home and family, depending on the hospitality and charity of friends. Yes, it turned out to be lucky for me to be a refugee. Out of adversity, often the most wonderful benefits arise.

[3]. Inscription from Socrates on the temple of Delphi.

5

Of Good Teachers II

In the preceding essay I wished to underline the immense influence teachers can have on the lives of human beings. Teaching is in my view one of the noblest, most beautiful and most important professions on earth.

The outstanding human quality of these two teachers was to arouse my enthusiasm (literally "by God possessed") and to unlock my passion for learning about the multiple manifestations of the miracle of life. As a result, I always remained a generalist, despite subsequent specialized studies. For other students a teacher may come along who arouses their interest for science, mathematics, history or literature, etc., and thus helps them to find their destiny and life fulfillment.

My mother, though, gave me a stern warning at the time. She used to say to me: "Son, you are too dispersed, too interested in everything, and as a result you will be truly knowledgeable in nothing. The world needs experts, specialists, professionals. I therefore predict to you that you will fail in life." She prevented me from learning music—the piano—and discouraged my love for painting. But when I see my mother in the afterworld, I will say to her:

"You were wrong after all. I continued to be interested in so many things that in the end I became a specialist in generalities! And the world happened to badly need generalists in the 1970s!"

So I was right to remain faithful to my basic inclinations and loves.[1]

I have only one complaint about the two exceptional educators who blessed my life: in retrospect, I would have liked them to communicate to me their passion in a spiritual context. I feel today that I have lost much time in finding my proper place in the realm of creation, namely that I myself, as any living being and particularly as a human, am an incredible cosmos, a miracle of magic complexity and perception, never to be repeated again exactly in all eternity; that I must love and relate well to my family, which is my own creation, to my neighbors, my town, my society and to the entire human family; that I must want to understand and love with all my heart the whole miraculous creation surrounding me: nature, its living beings and humanity's own achievements of good and beauty. But there remains one further immense circle to relate to: the fathomless, infinite universe and the incomprehensible stream of eternal time. That dimension is the realm of spirituality and God. Within it the human person seeks an answer to the most basic queries: why am I on earth, what is the meaning of my life? What is expected of me? A third teacher came along later who gave me the answer or reminded me of the one I had been given outside of school by my religion. He was U Thant, the Secretary-General of the United Nations, a former teacher in his country, Burma. He held that spirituality was the highest virtue and need of any human being. In spirituality he saw the mysterious conjunction between man's inner life and the universe, a harmony which alone can bring enlightenment, detachment, personal peace and

---

[1.] Regarding music and piano, my nontraining remained irreparable. Oh God, how much I would have loved to express in music my neverending passion and love for life! As regards painting, I definitely intend to return to it after my retirement.

bliss. To him, Socrates' "Know thyself" and Descartes' exclusive reliance on intelligence were severely handicapped, for they missed a cardinal point, namely our need to try to understand also with our heart and soul our correct place in the universe and in eternity.

It was not surprising, therefore, that in his memoirs he revealed the names of the three teachers who had most influenced his role as Secretary-General: Buddha, the teacher of life and death in the cosmos; Albert Schweitzer, the teacher of spirituality and action; and Teilhard de Chardin, the teacher of spirituality and science. U Thant was so sad whenever he saw a scheme for education which made no reference to spirituality. For him one of the most essential ingredients of education was spirituality in response to the hunger of the soul. Indeed, the human being is not made only of body and mind. The neglect of educating also the heart and the soul in many schools was for U Thant the greatest shortsightedness of our otherwise prestigious scientific and intellectual age. He simply could not understand it. Thus, in one of his farewell speeches when he left the United Nations (a speech to planetary Citizens) he said:

"What was my approach to all problems? It was the human approach. I attached the utmost importance to the human element in all problems: political, economic, social, racial, colonial or other. Some of you are aware of my philosophy regarding the human community and situation. In my view there are certain categories and priorities in values. I believe that an ideal man or an ideal woman is endowed with four virtues, four qualities: physical qualities, mental qualities, moral qualities and, above all, spiritual qualities. Of course, it is very rare to find a human being endowed with all these qualities. I attach importance to all of them, but I would attach greater importance to the mental or intellectual qualities over physical qualities. Still I would rate moral qualities higher than intellectual qualities. Still more, I would rate spiritual qualities the highest. It is far from my intention to downgrade or denigrate the physical and intellectual aspects of life. I am in no sense an anti-intellectual, but the stress of education in the schools of the highly developed societies, as I have stated on many previous occasions, is primarily on the development of the intellect or on physical excellence, without taking into account the moral and spiritual aspects of life. To me, the moral and spiritual aspects of life are far more important than the physical and intellectual aspects. That is why I have tried to develop, without perfection alas, those moral virtues and spiritual qualities like modesty, humility, love, compassion, the philosophy of live and let live, the desire to understand the other person's point of view, which constitute the keys to all great religions. . . ."

U Thant believed that peace on earth could be achieved only through proper education of the younger generations and that spirituality deserved the highest place in such education.[2] May the current concern for proper global education allow for spirituality, love and compassion to be given generous room in all the world's educational systems. It is in our highest interest to do so, if we want to stem war, violence, crime and unhappiness from endangering the peace, civilization and progress already achieved in our march toward optimum fulfillment of the miracle of life. May all educators heed these wise words of U Thant, one of the first global teachers and spiritual masters of the nascent world community:

[2] Toward the end of his mandate, Dag Hammarskjöld held a similar view when he said: "I see no hope for permanent world peace. We have tried and failed miserably. Unless the world has a spiritual rebirth, civilization is doomed."

The law of love and compassion for all living creatures is again a doctrine to which we are all too ready to pay lip service. However, if it is to become a reality, it requires a process of education, a veritable mental renaissance. Once it has become a reality, national as well as international problems will fall into perspective and become easier to solve. Wars and conflicts, too, will then become a thing of the past, because wars begin in the minds of men, and in those minds love and compassion would have built the defenses of peace.[3]

[3] From his speech, "Faith and Peace," delivered at the University of Toronto in October 1967. See "The Example of a Great Ethical Statesman: U Thant" in *Most of All, They Taught Me Happiness.*

6

Virtue Is
a Middle Course

During all your life, beware of extremes, of extremists and of watertight ideological systems.

The French lycée is a marvelous institution which forms, by the age of eighteen, full human beings equipped with the necessary knowledge, philosophy and mental means to face life in any circumstances. Thereafter begins specialization at university or in other institutions of higher learning. The lycée in my time produced happy and balanced individuals, perhaps with some overweight on knowledge and intelligence at the expense of character and qualities of the heart. The basic philosophy taught to us was typically French. It could be traced back to the Roman classical period: it was a philosophy of moderation, balance and personal equilibrium, with suspicion for all extremes as being contrary to humanistic culture. The great axioms were: *in medio stat virtus* (virtue is a middle course), *éviter les extrêmes* (to avoid the extremes), *les extrêmes se touchent* (extremes abut on each other). This golden rule of the middle had made France a happy and much admired country in the world. But it also rendered it extremely vulnerable to the Nazis. At the first shock, France crumbled and its people never really understood how this could have happened to them. Education was partly responsible, for one may well imagine that thousands of Frenchmen were reading literature, refusing to accept the idea of a war, and hoping for another Munich, when the conflict broke out. This explains why peaceful, moderate and humane nations cannot survive when there is a power-drunk, expansionist and military country around, unprepared to accept international law and rules of decency. It also explains why a strong United Nations is so important: the tighter an international system of reciprocal obligations and surveillance, the less likely political adventures of nations will be.

In 1940, the Nazis brought to Alsace-Lorraine among other evils their dictatorial system of education. What an experience that was! Their main objective was not to make decent human beings out of us, but to transform us into future führers, leaders for their totalitarian apparatus. The two main facets of that education were to make us believe in the universal superiority of the German culture (Goethe, Schiller, Beethoven, Bach, etc.) and in the virtues of German efficiency and unchallenged discipline (*Kadavergehorsam:* obedience unto death).

Our new masters taught us proudly about the wide gamut, depth and diversity or, as they called it, "the polarity" of the German being (*die Polarität des deutschen Wesens*). We were told that Germans—and we were of course "Germans by blood," whether we liked it or not!— had the capacity to switch at a moment's notice from one extreme to another without any internal conflict. Immense value and pride were attached to this Germanic characteristic, which stood in contrast with the narrow, classical, bourgeois, unimaginative and, as they called it, "decadent" equilibrium of the French!

The polarity of the German soul became well known during the war when the world heard stories of German family men, devoted to their wives and children, who turned into conscientious and systematic murderers of Jews, gypsies and other prisoners in concentration camps. The French author Robert Merle describes in his book *Death is My Profession* one of these *Bürgers*, who, being entrusted with the task of disposing of ever-increasing numbers of Jews, came up with the idea of burning them in their own fat in trenches along which other prisoners scooped up the melted grease to accelerate the process! He considered himself to be a good German trying to do his job as best as he could! After the war when he was brought to trial, he could not understand why his activities were being held against him. One shudders when one reads such documented stories. It is precisely this type of man, more refined and sophisticated, that Nazi education had in store for us.

I soon had an occasion to witness a firsthand example of what our teachers meant. During the summer vacations, all high school students were compelled to work in factories or on farms. I was assigned to a firm called Haffner in my hometown of Sarreguemines. Before the war it manufactured safes and now produced war material. I started to work as a helper at the lathes and was later transferred to the accounting department. The German director, R., took an interest in me, for he wanted to prove to me the unchallenged superiority of German efficiency and leadership. I was frequently called to his office and given practical lessons in German management. Thus, one morning, I was standing there, listening to his briefing when one of his subordinates reported that several Polish women who were working in the factory as forced labor had placed themselves on the sick list and that the toilets in their barracks were clogged. R. made his decision with lightning speed and without a moment's hesitation: the women would receive no food for two days and they were to unclog and clean the toilets with their bare hands. This would teach them a lesson! The whole scene lasted only a few seconds.

Then he suddenly remembered my presence, felt perhaps embarrassed, and sent me off abruptly, asking me to come to his home in the evening.

He lived not far from my parents' house in a beautiful villa called by the children "Candy Philippe's house" because it belonged before the war to a Philippe family, who had been candy manufacturers. The house had a magnificent orchard. After dinner, I went there and rang the bell. A stocky woman resembling a *Walküre* opened the door and told me that her husband was in the garden. I walked around the house and reached the orchard, where I heard the sound of music. I followed it until I saw R. sprawled out in an armchair in front of a radio. He stopped me with a brusque gesture of his hand, and I stood there in the dusk of the evening, under a warm summer sky filled with the piercing shrieks of swallows, surrounded by the fragrance of roses, listening to Beethoven's immortal Ninth Symphony, transmitted from Berlin under the baton of Wilhelm Furtwängler. My thoughts were lingering with the poor Polish women lying on their mattresses with empty stomachs, their minds probably filled with hatred for the Nazis and with images of their beloved ones in their faraway country.

The night had fallen when the symphony ended. R. switched off the radio. Long minutes of black, velvety silence dropped into eternity. He finally rose, turned his face toward me, wiped his eyes with a shirt sleeve and said:

"Müller, whenever I listen to Beethoven I end up crying with happiness!"

Polarity of the German soul. . . . Switching from one extreme to the other. . . . Polarity of human elation and human tears. . . . A man feeling like a supergod in his garden, and poor, hungry women in a barracks. . . . Tears of cultural superiority and cries of mothers separated from their children. . . . What kind of a human monster was that before me? Was he the same man who that morning condemned women to hunger and abjection? May God, I thought, spare the world any polarities of this sort and bless it with France's equilibrium, humanism and deep distrust for all extremes.

As an irony of fate, after the war, when R. was brought before an anti-Nazi tribunal in Saarbrücken, he named me as someone who could testify in his favor! I remembered that incident and told his lawyer that if I were to testify, I would probably not be a very favorable witness for his client.

I never met R. again. If I had, I would have thanked him for having unwittingly given me one of the most precious lessons in my life, namely that superiority and efficiency accompanied by cruelty and inhumanity can be a great curse for humanity. No end ever justifies immoral means. Only a madman like Hitler could say that "the fastest way to get to one's end, that is justice." Quite the contrary, evolution and the whole art of living are conciliation, adaptation, arbitration, mediation, understanding, reason, common sense within a same group, from the family to humanity, between groups and between our species and its planetary environment. How many times was I to remember that scene in my work at the United Nations, where the world's many cultures, groups, nations and ideologies still have not abandoned their game of intolerance and superiority.

He made me realize how education can be a distorting factor for humans on this planet. We had been taught most seriously by the French about the superiority of their culture, civilization, history, language, heroes, achievements and empire. Then came the Germans, who told us no less seriously with all the pomp, rationalism and scientism of education about the superiority of their "race," language, culture, efficiency, science, technology, political system and ideology, and tried to make us believe in their right to rule Europe and the world! How sacred, for instance, they considered the words "German blood," as if such nonsense existed. God has certainly not created humans with distinct national bloods! Humans existed for 2 to 3 million years on this planet before words like German, French, American or Russian were coined. No wonder that schools appear to me as sorts of "computer centers" where humans are being "wired in" with national values and superiorities while in reality the world is one, humanity is one, and the individual and humanity are greater realities than any nation. Hence the concentration of much of my writing on the need for a new education, a global education, a true world education.

Secretary-General U Thant, my beloved master, knew this well when, after ten years at the helm of the United Nations, he concluded that world peace, justice and happiness could be achieved only through a different education. How often did he tell me: "Robert, our own generation will not achieve world peace. For that, we need a new generation properly educated about the world, the human family and the supreme worth of the individual person." He felt that there was an urgent need, in a world divided by national interests, for an education which would teach each human being to give precedence to life, to the world and to humanity, reconciling citizenship with human allegiance, efficiency with humanism, and national objectives with world objectives. A journalist once asked him what in his view was the most important single obstacle to world peace. He answered that it was the principle "my country, right or wrong."

This is why he supported so wholeheartedly the first international schools on this planet and recommended the creation of a United Nations University. His dream became reality. "Give me your children, and I will give you the world." The university exists today, a milestone in human education and a bridge between scientists, the people and political leaders from all around the world. A few years later, the UNU was supplemented by the creation of a University for Peace in Costa Rica, one of the first countries in the world to have outlawed by constitution all armaments and military personnel. Remembering R., I derive great comfort from the fact that such progress was possible in my lifetime. A drive for proper global education everywhere will help prevent the recurrence of the inhuman regime and war I knew during my youth and which, in the middle of a civilized century and by the hands of a most advanced country, inflicted so much senseless misery and devastation on our beautiful planet.

7

The Berets

*Beware: Even the way of dressing can be used
to assert political divisions.*

When the Germans occupied Alsace-Lorraine in 1940, one
of their first actions was to prohibit the use of the French
language and the wearing of berets, a headgear which they
considered to be typically French.

The populations of the border areas were not basically
hostile to the Germans. Most of the people had German
names and traditions, and they spoke German rather than
French. Moreover they had just returned from a very pain-
ful evacuation and had lived through one of the most devas-
tating periods of French history. The people were glad to be
home again. The Germans were reconstructing the war-
damaged areas rapidly. Matters might therefore not have
been so bad for the Nazis had they not committed one of
those psychological blunders at which they were great experts, blinded as they were by their belief in indomitable
German superiority.

Yes, it was enough to prohibit French to see an almost
immediate flourishing of that language all over Alsace-Lorraine. The Nazis then took repressive measures. I remember that at first they introduced a fine of fifty pfennig (fifty
cents) when someone was caught speaking French. The
standard joke became to hand a one-mark bill (one dollar) to

the police, commenting: "Please keep the change. *Au revoir!*"

As for berets, people who would never have dreamed of wearing this headgear were looking for them everywhere in order to annoy the Germans. After our return home, my mother had reopened her milliner's shop and my father was again making hats. People came to both of them asking for berets. But my mother had never carried this item and my father was not equipped to produce it. Beret making is a specialty of the Basque region in southern France; hence the term "beret basque."

One day my mother told us that she had to satisfy her customers and that she would undertake a trip to Paris to buy berets. My father, who was a very timid man, did everything to dissuade her, but in vain. She had firmly made up her mind.

During the first months after the German occupation it was still relatively easy to travel from Alsace-Lorraine to France, although the 1914 borders had been reestablished. Customs and exchange controls were severe, but my mother, like many people living on borders, was a consummate smuggler. Smuggling was for us a challenge against nationalism, an exercise in imagination, a real art, and we used every occasion and conceivable trick to fool customs control. For example, when I was an infant, my mother used to smuggle brandy for my father into Belgium by putting into my mouth a bottle of liquor wrapped up in a diaper and topped by a nipple without a hole!

So, she left one day for France with a few thousand francs rolled up tightly and hidden in the back of a book. She intended to leave the book on a seat of the train compartment during customs control. "If the money should by extraordinary bad fortune be found," she said, "I can always claim that the book did not belong to me and that someone else left it there."

She stayed in Paris for several days and we were anxiously awaiting her return. My father, who by nature was very nervous about such adventures—which my mother on the contrary adored—was going out of his mind. Finally we received a telegram from Paris announcing her return and asking us to meet her at the railroad station at a specified time.

It was evening and raining. My father was nervously pacing up and down the platform until the train arrived. We watched the doors open, saw my mother emerge from one of the compartments and hurried toward her to help her carry two enormous cartons. The strings of the heavy packages were cutting our palms. My father covered my mother with reproaches instead of rejoicing at her return and asking her how she had fared. As we were stumbling with our load toward the station's exit, I asked her:

"How on earth did you manage to carry these sizable cartons when you changed trains in Metz and how did you get through the German customs?"

She looked at me as if I was the biggest imbecile on earth and with her magnificent clear blue eyes piercing me, she answered superbly:

"I asked two German soldiers to help me. They accompanied me through customs very gallantly, carrying the two packages, which the customs officials under the circumstances did not inspect!"

When we arrived home we opened the cartons: they contained a few hundred brand-new berets, each of them a symbol of French freedom and of defiance against Nazi totalitarianism!

And thus I learned that even such elementary things as civilian clothes can be used and fought over by nations to assert their identities and value preferences. As Voltaire said, hordes of people have slaughtered one another throughout history simply because they wore hats on one side and turbans on the other. Sometimes I feel that if I wanted to make a fortune I could leave the United Nations and start a new profession called "entity promotion." It would go far beyond public relations or advertising. I would say to my customers, "You want to promote an entity? A race, a religion, an institution, a nation, a minority, a firm, an interest group, a product, a service—anything, you name it. I will tell you how to do it." For, over the years at the UN, I have gathered files on that game. The first deals with every possible technique to prove that your entity is superior: you need a flag, a hymn, an education, a creed, a protocol, a language, monuments, famous persons, heroes, martyrs, a history, an art, if possible arms and even special ways of dressing! My second file deals with ways to diminish other entities: lie about them, denigrate them, do not cease to repeat that they are bad, accuse them of anything and everything, say that their products, history, literature, art, system, culture, etc., are decadent or inferior to yours, call them by any names you can find and even state that their way of dressing is primitive and distasteful!

The human species still plays these games widely over the planet, although through travel, communications, international education and exchange of information, increasing numbers of people are getting wise to it. True enough, we need entities. They are a fact of life, a biological, philosophical and practical necessity. The question is, how can they be made truthful, effective and harmonious for the benefit of the entire human race? Humanity has not even begun to study that problem. One of my strongest recommendations to social scientists would be to have a close look at the play and interplay of entities and at the mediation and solution of problems and conflicts between them. It is revealing that the Chinese words for government mean "putting things at their right place"—our right place on this planet, our right place in relation to each other and our right place in the universe and in time. The Buddhists give us another possible answer: unity in diversity. Let us be diverse, by all means, down to each individual human person, dressing differently, eating differently, loving differently, cherishing our cultural and folkloric diversity, but not letting these differences become the source and instruments of hatred, divisions and wars. Human dressing habits, like uniforms, are a much more deep-seated problem than I had thought at first. They can perhaps give us valuable clues to some of the fundamental aspects of human nature and behavior.

One can ask oneself, for example, the question what someday the uniforms, flags, symbols, monuments, hymns, customs, language, literature, art, history, heroism and clothes of a unified, free, democratic, interdependent world society will be? In which direction are we moving? What will be the end result? Who will exercise the main influence? What should we want and who will decide? In this search I would most seriously commend to the attention of social and political scientists the examples of Switzerland, Confucianism and Buddhism as possible answers to the societal problems of this planet.

8

An Aborted
Barge Trip

Democracy is the worst system, except all others.

Churchill

Summer 1941. The Germans had been occupying Alsace-Lorraine for more than a year and they were impatient to integrate the population fully into the German Reich despite the protests of Marshal Pétain, who argued that Alsace-Lorraine should remain French until a peace treaty was signed. Local life was almost completely Germanized, except for our passports and identification papers, which bore the label *Volksdeutscher Elsässer or Lothringer,* i.e., Alsatian or Lorrainer of German stock. At school a full-swing campaign was being waged to enroll volunteers into the German army. One of my classmates, a tall, handsome seventeen-year-old boy who dreamed of becoming a pilot, volunteered and was killed within a year. Among the population the rumor spread that a draft into the German army would be decreed soon, and some young men began to cross the border to France.

The first measure the Germans took was to enlist us into the Arbeitsdienst, or work service—a paramilitary corps invented by Hitler to give young men an almost complete military training, except for weapons. Instead of rifles, they used shiny spades for drills and exercises. After the Arbeitsdienst, at the age of eighteen, a young man entering the German army could be turned into a full-fledged soldier within a few weeks.

The Arbeitsdienst was also used, in my opinion, as a means to eliminate the physically unfit and to improve "genetically" the German race. Thus, during the winter of 1941–42, we learned that several of our young men had died of pneumonia in that service. No wonder! They had been forced to jump naked into ice-cold ponds or rivers and to swim. Those who fell sick and died were simply unfit to belong to the German race! When I remember such horrors, I often wonder why humanity is not happier today, now that such atrocities and encroachments upon human life have been eliminated from most countries, thanks especially to a constant and vigilant battle for human rights. And I wonder also why people do not support the United Nations more, the only organization on earth where there is at least the beginning of a chance to denounce and to combat the internal horrors so often committed by nations.

The question arose in my family as it did in so many others: would I go to the Arbeitsdienst and later most certainly to the German army or would I escape to France? The perennial drama repeated itself in our borderland: educated in the French humanistic tradition, we would soon be asked and later forced to join Nazi-German organizations designed to kill our brethren in the name of an insane group ideology.

In such cases, the family point of view usually prevailed. It is true, some young men left without discussing the matter with their parents, leaving them to their unfortunate fate. But in most cases the question was fully debated, since the consequences affected the entire family. Fearing a mass exodus, the Germans were preparing drastic measures against the relatives of the so-called *réfractaires.* The rumor was widely spread, surely by the Germans themselves, that their families would be deported to Poland or to the Sudetenland.

In my family, the situation was as follows: two of my three cousins who had reached military age joined the German army and one escaped to France. In one family, the two brothers were split: one joined the First French Army in North Africa and the other became a German soldier. As for me, my father took from the very beginning a firm, crystal-clear and highly emotional decision. He said to me: "Under no circumstances will I allow you to wear the German uniform." This reminded me of his prewar statement that if the Germans ever came back, he would pack his toothbrush and pajamas and leave for France.

Ironically enough, he had said these words in German, since his French was rather poor. His verdict was based on the conviction that no one should ever help the Germans win the war. His view was that France, despite all its deficiencies and disorder, was infinitely superior to Germany with all its order, discipline and efficiency, for it was a humane country which left its people in peace and free to do what they wanted. He shared Churchill's view that democracy is the worst possible system, except all others. The age-old issue was indeed that of order and freedom and the delicate balance between the two. My father's good common sense and simplicity taught me more about this fundamental human dilemma than all the learned treatises painstakingly elaborated by writers and political scientists.

Alas, when the Germans overran France, there was no longer any other place to go to and my father could not take his suitcase, pajamas and toothbrush and leave for his country of choice. But he remained firm as a rock on the question of his son's uniform and refused to discuss the consequences it could have for the family. He made his own inquiries regarding the ways and means by which I could escape to France and one day he came home with an answer:

"I want you to pack a few belongings and leave for the town of Thionville in the north of Lorraine where you will cross the border, hidden on a barge navigating between Lorraine and France on the Moselle River."

He told me that a good friend of his, a baker named Guehl, had two brothers in Thionville. One was a baker too, the other a barge owner. I would live for a few days with the baker's family until the brother could take me across the border.

I took leave of my parents and traveled by train to Thionville, where I was welcomed by a very nice and warm family. They took me to visit a river barge used for the transport of coal. Under the heaps of coal a little wooden shack had been built where a person could hide for a few hours until the border was crossed. I was given all the details concerning the crossing, which would take place in a few days, and I also spent some time in the hideout in order to get accustomed to the claustrophobic conditions.

As I was waiting for the day of crossing, a telegram suddenly came from my father asking me to return home. It gave no explanations.

When I arrived home, he told me the following:

"During the last few days I happened to become acquainted with a German from the Rhineland, a man named Peters, a very devout Catholic who hates the Nazis and who works in the local civilian administration. We had a lot of beers and brandies together, and at one point I told him of my wish to see you cross the border to avoid joining the German army. He retorted that this was utter foolishness at this stage, as they had received orders to prepare for the deportation of the families of all young men who would refuse to join the Arbeitsdienst. He said that enlistment in that work service was not such a serious problem compared with the army and that he could easily obtain for you a deferral for study purposes. He is a member of the Drafts Committee. All you have to do is to pass the medical examination and you will be automatically deferred. He begged me to stop you from escaping to France at this stage. He strikes me as a good, very religious and warm-hearted man, and I am sure that he would not tell me lies. In any case, should they ever draft you, you will still have the option of crossing the border as planned."

I obeyed my father and presented myself to the review committee. I still remember how badly I felt when a young man sitting next to me refused to undress to take the medical examination. The Germans quickly surrounded him and asked:

"Why do you refuse to undress?"

"Because you do not have the right to enlist me in a German organization."

"Why not?"

"Because I am French."

"*Ach ja?* But how come that you said it in German?"

They arrested him quickly to prevent any movement of solidarity from the other young men. I heard a Nazi predict to him that after a few days of solitary confinement he would discover in the depth of his heart how good a German he was!

I was a little ashamed that I had my own way out of the situation. When my turn came at the Drafts Committee I saw Mr. Peters hand a slip of paper to the chairman. The latter informed me that I had been deferred until the following year in order to allow me to begin graduate studies at the University of Heidelberg. I walked out of the room with a certificate to that effect in my hand.

This first accommodation with the circumstances, followed by several others, avoided the deportation of my family. Nothing could have been less heroic, but today I am grateful and happy that thanks to a good German my family was spared and that we survived one of the greatest and most insane political adventures the world has ever seen.

O God, by what miracle am I still alive forty-five years later, while so many of my friends are dead? I almost do not dare to return to my hometown for fear of meeting the eyes of their mothers, who silently seem to ask: "Why is he alive and not my son?" How could I have dreamed at the time that I would work some day for the United Nations? Dear God, your ways are indeed mysterious. You must have had a reason. Will you explain it to me?

God: "Yes, my son. I spared you so that you could work with all your strength, all your heart and all your soul for peace in the world. Never forget that of all the little boys with whom you played in your neighborhood, you are the only one alive. Remember the eyes of their mothers. You owe the living and the dead quite a special life. You must absolutely help prevent the return of similar senseless, inhuman, sacrilegious, heartbreaking and unforgivable killings on the beautiful planet I created in the universe."

9

Of Glasses

Personal freedom and ingenuity are not vain words.

August 1942. The Nazi governors of Alsace and Lorraine had decreed that all young men of eighteen were to serve in the German army. I had enjoyed for more than a year my deferral from the Arbeitsdienst and was about to enter my second year of studies in economics at the University of Heidelberg.

My father consulted his friend Peters about the situation. Peters had no influence over the military and there was little he could do. He thought that the only way out for me was to obtain a low health classification and another deferral for study purposes. He continued to be firmly opposed to my crossing the border, since he felt that the war would still last for quite some time until Hitler was defeated. I should escape only as a means of last resort and avoid as long as possible the deportation of my parents. But I was in splendid health and my only physical handicap was my nearsightedness, which forced me to wear glasses. Peters concentrated on that aspect:

"Do you know anyone who could discreetly obtain for your son thicker glasses than those he is wearing?"

My father thought it over for a moment and said:

"Yes. I could talk to my friend and business neighbor Welters, a medical supplies merchant from whom we have always been buying the glasses for my son. I will see what I can do."

Welters agreed readily:

"I have a small supply of blank prescription forms from Dr. X., the former ophthalmologist who did not return to our town after the Germans came. I can forge his signature and fill out a prescription with a prewar date. My producer in Götzenbruck will deliver to me the glasses corresponding to the higher dioptries. Such direct orders are quite customary when someone breaks his glasses and does not want to pay for another consultation."

On the day of the medical review I was wearing these new, thicker glasses. They were so strong that I could hardly see through them. When it came to the eyesight examination, a German sergeant proceeded as follows:

"Take your glasses off and read the letters on the wall."

I could not read anything.

He marked down something on a sheet of paper and said:

"Now put your glasses on and read."

I could barely read any better, for the glasses were too strong! I walked a few steps nearer, straining my eyes in order to read the text.

"Good," said the sergeant.

I handed him the prescription, from which he copied the dioptries, and he commented: "Your glasses are not strong enough!" He then put on his most intelligent face, concentrated on some savant calculations and . . . added a few dioptries to his report!

When the major in charge of the final examination saw that report, he looked at me with surprise and said:

"My poor lad, how can you study with such bad eyes?"

I answered meekly:

"It is hard, indeed, but I try to manage."

"I feel sorry for you. You are strong and healthy otherwise, but I cannot pronounce you fit for active service on account of your bad eyesight. You would shoot your neighbor instead of your enemy. All I can do is to classify you as GvH *(Garnisonsverwändungsfähig-Heimat,* i.e., fit for garrison duty in the rear), and the best service I can render the German army is to defer you altogether and allow you to return to university."

I left the Kommandantur with another deferral sheet and a certificate of physical unfitness in my pocket! Peters had won again. I had only one question on my mind:

"Had all this been prearranged with the complicity of Peters or was it really a blunder by the German sergeant?"

Peters denied vehemently having had any part in the affair. He ascribed it fully to Nazi military stupidity:

"They are so blinded by their belief in superiority and infallibility that sagacity and discrimination have died out almost completely from their brains."

I thought for myself that indeed such a crude ruse would have never succeeded with a French military review board.

One of the great pleasures in this matter was of course the victory of a small group of men—my father, his two friends and I—in fooling the enormous apparatus of a totalitarian state! Personal freedom and ingenuity are after all not vain words.

10

An Appendectomy

Autosuggestion can lead to health as well as to sickness.

Spring 1943. Our good friend Peters warned my father that drafting into the German army was being accelerated, since Hitler needed every man he could lay his hands on. My low health classification no longer protected me and I would undoubtedly be included in the next batch of draftees. Persuaded that the Nazis would lose the war, Peters persisted in giving the same advice:

"Do not do anything foolish. Gain time. Try by all means to survive this insane war."

He came up with another idea and asked my father:

"Can you trust your family doctor, Dr. Friedrich, who is also a surgeon?"

"Yes. We are intimate friends. We come from the same village and our families were very close to each other."

"That is good. Could you then ask him to take your son in treatment for a possible operation, such as an appendectomy? He has to take every measure to make it look real. I will be able to learn the date of dispatch of the next drafts and I will advise you in time so that your son can be in the hospital when the postman delivers the order. That will save him probably for another two or three months."

Dr. Friedrich agreed readily and took all possible precautions: he arranged for several visits to his office, showed me exactly where the appendix was located, advised me to press hard on that spot every day and sent me to Dr. Bouton, a radiologist and close friend of his. There I had to drink a thick, nauseating calcium milk to fill my intestines and have X-rays taken. Dr. Bouton concluded and certified that there was strong suspicion of an infected appendix.

I returned to the University of Heidelberg and pressed every day very hard on my abdomen. The spot became quite sensitive after a while and I was able through systematic autosuggestion to persuade myself that I had appendicitis.

Then, one Friday, I received a telegram from my father asking me to come home. I knew what that meant. The following morning I was in the hospital being operated on by Dr. Friedrich.

It was the first operation I'd had in my life. The anesthesia in particular left a very deep impression on me. I remember vividly every effect it caused. A *braune Schwester* had been assigned to me. These Nazi nurses, dressed in brown uniforms, had replaced the Catholic sisters who had been expelled from the hospital when the Nazis came. Schwester Erika was a very good-looking, healthy German girl who under any other regime would have been quite a lovable woman. But she had gone through the BdM (Bund Deutscher Mädchen), the League of German Girls, a feminine counterpart of the Hitlerjugend, and she was trying very hard to look, think and act like a strong, heartless, efficient woman-soldier, devoted only to the Reich, her Führer and the war effort.

I will never forget her air of suspicion and her rough-handling when she shaved my abdomen before the operation. She did not stop asking me questions: what symptoms I had, where exactly I had pains, what kind of pains. I jumped and shouted whenever she touched the precise spot, trying to catch me unaware. But I had learned my lesson well and I was really feeling pain.

She wheeled me to the operating room and gave me anesthesia by means of ether dropping on a mask over my mouth and nose. She asked me to count. My wheel-bed was standing near a washbasin in a room adjoining the operating room. From a faucet drops of water were falling into the basin. As I was counting under her grinning but beautiful face, the sound of the drops became louder and louder. I closed my eyes and saw colorful circles expanding into ever-wider, infinite dimensions. Each drop was more resounding than the preceding one and echoed like a gigantic gong hit by a slave. Colossal circles, colors and sounds seemed to reverberate in the universe. Each time I thought that the extreme limits of noise, light and distance had been reached, but what followed was even vaster. Never in my life had I experienced such extreme perceptions. For the first time I had the distinct feeling that the concepts of infinity and eternity are within the reach of the human person and that beyond our "prosaic," normal daily life there is a stunning world of unsuspected, Promethean perceptions unlocked by chemicals and hallucinogens.

When I woke up, Sister Erika was holding my hand and interrogating me. She was asking me questions about my studies, my political opinions, my appendicitis and Dr. Friedrich. But I had expected it before the operation and I had brainwashed myself to satiety with the conviction that my appendix was sick, that I had had to undergo surgery and that I was in terrible pain.

Apparently I did not do so badly. Dr. Friedrich entered my room to tell me with a broad grin that he had removed an enormous, beautifully infected appendix:

"It was on the verge of rupture and you would have been in great danger if it had not been removed."

The week that followed was truly delightful: my parents and many friends visited me. I was spoiled, especially by the local teenage girls, since I was one of the very few boys of their age left in the town. I still possess a picture of a group of exquisite young girls who brought me books and flowers. This infuriated the *braune Schwester*, who, being now convinced of the authenticity of my need for surgery, liked to come herself and spend long moments at my bedside, discussing philosophy, literature and politics. She could not stand these young girls from the local bourgeoisie, whom she called *"dumme Gänse"* (stupid geese). She considered that I had a good mind and that my ambitions should reach beyond my little town. I liked her company too. In our conversations I often came back to my anesthesia and I asked these questions stubbornly:

"Where does life end and death begin? Which is the infinitesimal but enormously significant droplet of ether which 'kills' and makes the gigantic difference between life and death? What happens exactly at that precise moment or infinitesimal small speck of time? Until that moment our colossal human being or cosmos made up of trillions of cells, miles of vessels and hundreds of automatic mechanisms, all working miraculously together, can 'come back' to its normal, stupendous functioning, but one more drop will end it for all eternity, without any chance of 'return'! What a quantum effect that little drop has! Or is it not possible that there is no discontinuity at all between life and death, that matter, or what we call matter, is simply changing its form and pursuing an endless course of transformation in the universe? Or is it life itself or a 'soul' which is migrating from one form to another? Death is perhaps a misunderstanding by humans, bearing little relation to the infinitely more fundamental realities of the universe. Being already unconscious, what more could have happened to me at the moment when the 'decisive' droplet of ether would have tipped me over from 'life' to 'death'? I was already 'gone,' unconscious, totally insensitive to my environment. The surrounding world was dead for me. And yet I still 'lived'! What momentous, gigantic effect was taking place at the instant of that droplet? At what point precisely would I have been 'dead' or would my 'soul' have left my human envelope, as the Hindus think it does?"

She had no answer to these questions but told me about similar narcotic reactions of patients she had known.

The *braune Schwester* visited me ever more frequently, especially in the evenings after her tour of duty. I began to like her very much. Behind her stern appearance and almost military gait, there was a marvelous, intelligent and warm woman, beating with all the loving impulses of life. The military, the toughness had been added only superficially by education. No regime can really change the fundamental nature, warmth and uniqueness of a human being. It is that true, profound being which is being sought by another person and consecrated by the feeling of love.

It was high time for me to leave the hospital. A few days after my release, I brought Erika a bouquet of flowers and she invited me for a tête-à-tête dinner in her room at the hospital. We spent the evening together talking philosophy and trying once more to find what held the world together. When I left, we looked at each other for a long, very long moment and our eyes said many moving things to each other. But our lips remained silent and apart, for we knew that we belonged to different worlds. I never saw her again and today, after so many years, I wonder what has become of her, where she might be on this planet, and what fate God had in store for her. May He have been good to her and brought her much peace, love and happiness. She well deserved it, as does every human being.

This reminiscence of Erika, the *braune Schwester*, made me almost forget to say that when the draft notice for the German army arrived at my home, I was in the hospital and I was deferred for another few months.

After the war, Dr. Friedrich assured me that my appendix had really been infected and that I would have needed an urgent operation at any moment. He said to me: "I seldom saw such a thick, beautifully diseased appendix. It was heaven-sent to me, because the Nazis were very suspicious at the large number of appendectomies being performed in Alsace-Lorraine. A Gestapo man attended the operation. I could not believe my eyes when I saw and extracted your appendix. Was it mere coincidence or the result of your autosuggestive practices?[1] I will never know."

He told me dreadful stories of how young men from our region had mutilated themselves in order to avoid the German army.

"Some of them broke a leg or an arm with an iron bar. You can imagine how many times it took until they succeeded in breaking bones of such strength!"

His own nephew, L.L., a classmate of mine, had joined the German army but after a first tour of duty on the Russian front he had asked his uncle for help. The doctor resorted to an old trick from World War I: he injected into his nephew's leg a few cubic centimeters of turpentine. This produced a putrefying infection which lasted for several months and kept the young man away from the front. After the war, L.L. showed me his leg and an enormous cavity in

---

[1.] Autosuggestion can lead to health and to sickness, as was proved so brilliantly by Dr. Coué in his famous, classic *Self-mastery Through Conscious Auto-suggestion*. I can also add the example of former Secretary-General U Thant: whenever he did not want to go on an official trip abroad, he managed to get sick through autosuggestion.

it. He commented: "Better a hole in the leg than in the head." Such was, indeed, the philosophy of many Alsace-Lorrainers at that time. To live or not to live, that was the question.

11

Crossing the Border

Never ignore the warnings of extrasensory perceptions.

Summer 1943. The time had come to seriously consider crossing the border with France and to do it well in advance of the time when the Germans would issue their new wave of draft notices.

A friend of mine from Metz, L., who was also studying at the University of Heidelberg, decided to join me in my attempt.

We were confronted with three main problems: how to plan the escape in a manner that would entail the least risk of deportation or imprisonment for our families; how to succeed; and how to find a way out in case we were arrested. We examined all these points very carefully and agreed to the following dispositions.

Since neither of us had a draft notice to the army, we decided to give the escape the appearance of a students' escapade to Paris, avoiding every indication that it was a refusal to serve in the German army. The summer vacations were near. The next notices would be issued in September. If we were caught crossing the border, we could try to make the whole affair look like a summer excursion to Paris.

Secondly, if the escape succeeded, our parents would need an alibi for our disappearance. The explanations they would have to give to the Nazis needed at least to create some doubts in their minds to forestall a deportation. We planned, therefore, a mountain climbing expedition in the Austrian Alps, during which we could have been killed and disappeared. The scheme was very crude, but it would give our parents a little respite from being molested forthwith.

Finally, since L. was from Metz, a city very near the border, his father would try to find a *passeur*, one of those men who had sprung up during the war to help people cross the border for a fee.

To build up our case for a "Paris excursion," we took a series of measures, such as the renewal of our room rentals in Heidelberg and registration for the next semester, and we deposited a good amount of money in our German savings accounts. We would carry the bankbooks with us when we went to France.

L.'s father was able to find a *passeur* and a date was set for the crossing. We packed our luggage and left for our diversionary trip to Austria. It was my first visit to that country and strangely enough it has remained one of the greatest blanks in my memory. All I remember is that when we arrived in Vienna at dawn, after a sleepless night in an overcrowded German train, we ate goulash for breakfast at the station! I cannot even remember the name of our hotel, I have no idea how many days we stayed in Vienna and I have no recollection whatever of the city. Our main occupation was to write letters to our parents informing them that we were buying mountain climbing equipment and that we would leave in a few days for the Austrian Alps. We entrusted the last letters to French girls who worked as maids in the hotel. They were to post them in a specific order over a period of days after our departure.

For the return trip to Metz we took a sleeping car in order to be in fresh physical condition for the crossing. I still remember one detail of that trip: while the train had halted at a station, early in the morning, the sounds of a brass band woke us up suddenly. We dressed, opened the window and saw in front of us a Nazi band playing a fanfare. We were in Stuttgart. When the band stopped playing, a woman detached herself from the group of Nazis and brought a big bouquet of flowers to a lady standing at the window next to ours. We learned that she was Pilar Primo de Rivera, the sister of the Spanish fascist who had founded the famous "Blue Division," which was fighting for the Germans on the Russian front.

When we arrived in Metz, bad news awaited us: the *passeur* who was to take us across the border had been arrested and L.'s father had not been able to find another one. Until further notice we would stay with my uncle, Marcel Muller, a baker in the Rue des Allemands. For nearly two weeks we were secluded in a room on the first floor above the bakery, to avoid being seen since we were supposed to be in Austria. At long last my uncle found another *passeur*, a certain Bernard from Montigny-les-Metz. Half of the sum for the crossing was paid to his intermediary, a girl called Yvonne, the other half being payable after a safe crossing. My mother came to see me and to wish me godspeed. At the last minute she stuffed warm underwear and a big chunk of smoked ham into my small suitcase.

We left Metz for a locality to the north called St. Privat. At the station, Yvonne, the girl friend of the *passeur*, was waiting for us and for two other passengers, a woman and a young man of military age. We all went to a nearby restaurant where we became acquainted with each other and waited for the *passeur*. He arrived later during the evening. He was a wiry, redheaded, squirrel-like, nervous chap. He guided us to the woods where three other persons, a young man and an adult couple were waiting. Then began a long journey of several kilometers through woods and fields toward the French border. For a good part of the way we walked on an abandoned railroad track, a very tiring exercise, for the traversing beams were too close for one step and a little too far apart for a step to each second beam. The young man with whom I had become acquainted at the restaurant was walking behind me as the last person in the column. I helped him carry his suitcase part of the way, since my own luggage, designed for a "short vacation in Paris," as I told him, was very light.

The night was bright and beautiful, illuminated by a magnificent full moon which covered the silent landscape with a rare, transparent blue gauze. Underneath, the earth was pulsating, warm and fragrant like the voluptuous body of a woman. I wondered once more in my life why we had to walk like thieves or criminals on an earth which belonged to all people. Why were there borders? Why were there fences and walls? Why were there arms to defend those human corrals called nations? Later, the pictures brought back by the astronauts from outer space indeed showed that there were no borders on earth.

Our redheaded scout passed the word when we crossed the border during the interval between two German patrols. For a minute we became even more silent, living within our own thoughts and emotions. The date was 15 August 1943, the feast of the Holy Virgin.

When we were far into French territory, the *passeur* gathered us in a wheat field on the outskirts of a village and said:

"You are safe now. In the morning you can take a train from here to the interior of France. If you want to spend the rest of the night sleeping, you can go to that barn over there, near the first farmhouse. The peasants are accustomed to such nocturnal visits. I myself will return to Metz and inform your relatives of our successful crossing. Good luck to you all."

The adult couple and the woman went to that barn. The young man with whom I had become acquainted said that he would go to the village, borrow a bicycle and ride to his uncle's place in a neighboring village. L., myself and the third young man, an escapee from the German army, decided to hide in the wheat field until morning. We said good-bye to each other and the group disbanded.

Bales of freshly cut wheat were scattered over the field. We put several of them together in the form of tepees so as to provide us with convenient sleeping and hiding places. In order not to rumple my only suit, I took it off and put on two or three additional undershirts and briefs which my mother had placed in my suitcase at the last moment.

My two companions soon began to snore, but I could not sleep. The moon was too beautiful, the air too crisp, the bales of wheat too fragrant and my heart too full of thoughts, images and concern for the fate of my beloved ones. Between the infinite sky and my insignificant being hidden in the wheat stacks a myriad of intense relations and feelings were alive. Finally, after a good night's prayer to the Lord, worn out by the tenseness of the day, I was about to close my eyes and to fall asleep when suddenly a feeling that I had never experienced before in my life took possession of my whole being. A powerful, internal voice was warning and pressing me. An external force was almost shaking me:

"Get up and run away from here as fast as you can. Do it right away, do not wait a moment, do not think, flee. . . ."

The voice and the feeling were pounding on me with incredible strength. My heart was beating wildly, sending gushes of hot blood to my head. But my brain asserted itself and held the following language:

"This feeling is nonsense, irrational, entirely without foundation. The crossing of the border has been successful, we are miles inside of France and there is not a human soul or sound in the whole neighborhood. If the Germans could have arrested us, they would have done it at the moment when we crossed the border and when the *passeur* was with us."

I obeyed this rational dictate of my mind, for I had been trained to be logical and intelligent, but the feeling was still there, impatient and powerful, almost tangible. Yes, it was like being touched by an invisible force or presence. Then, after a while, it subsided, as if it knew that I would not obey and that it was too late anyway.

I could not go to sleep. Nailed to my hiding place by my logic, all my other senses were acutely on the alert, knowing perfectly well that something was going to happen and that my brain had been stupid and wrong. I was calm and reconciled to my fate, just waiting for the event to occur.

After a while, which seemed an eternity, I heard light crackling sounds on the wheat field all around me. My two companions were snoring peacefully. The moon was watching the scene, impassive, imperturbable. The crickets all of a sudden became silent. The steps came closer and closer until a loud, beastly voice broke out in the silence of the night:

"*Heraus, sie Schweinehunde. Hände hoch.*" (Get out, you pigs' dogs. Hands up.)

I arose and saw our spot surrounded by half a dozen Gestapo men dressed in dark leather uniforms, revolvers in their hands and holding two big German shepherds by the leash. The policemen kicked my two bewildered companions out of their hiding place, examined our faces with flashlights, asked us for our identification papers, ordered us to dress and handcuffed us. To the third young man who was with us, the commanding Gestapo man said:

"We know you. You failed to return to your regiment after your leave. I have the sad honor to inform you that you were awarded the *Eiserne Kreuz* [iron cross] for your good behavior on the Russian front."

Turning to us, after having examined our papers, he said:

"Trying to fly away from the German army, you young birds, eh?"

I snapped back:

"You have no right to say that. We were on our way to Paris where we wanted to have a vacation, that is all."

He broke out in loud laughter and said:

"Nice story. We will see if you can make it stick."

From the exchanges of remarks I overheard between the Gestapo men, I concluded that we were small fry for them. They were disappointed not to find any American or British pilots as well as not to have laid hands on the *passeur*.

Two black limousines were driven up to the road alongside the wheat field. We were shoved into them and taken to the prison of St. Privat. Before leaving the grounds I had a last avid look at this little place of earth, at the tranquil landscape, at the moon, at the soil of France and at the strange spot where I had experienced my first extrasensory perceptions. I swore to God that if the mysterious forces ever came back to warn me of an impending danger, I would silence my mind forthwith and obey their injunctions, however irrational they might be.

And they came back, many times in later years— enough of them to fill an entire volume. Without that dramatic experience during the war, I might not have paid attention to them. There was probably need for an acute danger to arouse me to a capacity which otherwise might have remained dormant all my life. This, at least, is what I thought at that time. It was the beginning of a mysterious but very real facet of my life, which gained in intensity as the years passed.

Today, after many years of observation, I don't believe that it is a capacity inherent in certain persons. I am rather inclined to believe that there are spirits "alive" around us, good spirits and evil ones. The good ones try to give us signals in their own way, but usually we do not look out for them. In certain cases of extreme danger they almost succeed in becoming physical or exercising physical effects: they shake us, they make us see, hear or feel something; they accelerate our heartbeat; they try to make us run away from an impending danger. Extrasensory perceptions may therefore be a misnomer dating from the scientific, rational age. Instead of being a "capacity," they may be spiritual warnings by the still "living" souls of persons who love us, who follow us, who see what will happen to us, of a dead father or mother, a grandfather or grandmother, a peacemaker, a saint or an artist who want us to live and to continue their work. My life is filled with such spiritual signs. I am alert to them and I record them carefully. I am deeply intrigued by a phenomenon which is increasing in intensity all over the globe and which may be part of the spiritual transcendence and increased sensitivity of the human species to a world yet unknown to us.[1]

[1] I was struck by the statement of Edgar D. Mitchell, former Apollo 14 astronaut: "There are no unnatural nor supra-natural phenomena, only very large gaps in our knowledge of what is natural. We should strive to fill those gaps of ignorance."

12

A Couple of Prisons

Must we lose something to really appreciate it?

We spent only a few hours in the prison of St. Privat, a typical small-town jail. We could not communicate with each other and the only positive thing I found to do was to undress and to try to get rid of my triple underwear. What my mother had stuffed into my suitcase at the last moment was enough to suggest a winter expedition to the North Pole rather than a summer excursion to Paris! But where could I hide these garments? After a thorough search I found an opening in the plaster ceiling where the heating pipes penetrated into the upper floor of the building. The hole was small enough not to attract attention and large enough to allow me to press with a finger my surplus underwear into the empty space above the ceiling. I can visualize the puzzlement which these garments must have caused to workers reconditioning or tearing down the building years later, unless they served in the meantime, in shredded form, as nesting materials for rats and mice!

At dawn a prison van came to fetch us and we were transferred to the Gestapo in Metz. This was a much more dreadful affair. The prison consisted of a series of cellars in an apartment building which the Gestapo was using as its headquarters. In my cell there were at times up to thirty prisoners, while the room had sleeping accommodations for only four. A small cellar window opening on a courtyard was the only source of air. A bucket in a corner served as the toilet and smelled appallingly. The prisoners had nothing to do except wait for the footsteps of a guard coming to fetch someone for interrogation. There was little talk among the prisoners, as if they knew that conversation and agitation would only deplete the scarce oxygen in the cell. I have described in a chapter of *Most of All, They Taught Me Happiness* how I overcame this dreadful situation, using the grand old recipe of Dr. Coué, which has helped me so many times in my life. I kept my mind outside the prison and spent hours writing on the door of the cell a novel unfolding in snow-covered, sunlit and oxygen-drenched mountains.

Imprisonment is a great test in the art of living: one can see the walls, the ugliness, the darkness, the misery, the despair, the loss of freedom, but one can also concentrate on one's mind and heart, on the image of a beloved person, a flower, a souvenir, the moment of recovered freedom, one's future plans for life. Sometimes I think that to be really happy in this world and to appreciate life a person must have been imprisoned. We are so badly educated that we have to lose something to value it really. It is the greatest lesson on earth. It taught me to be grateful for my innumerable daily blessings, which I had taken too much for granted. Since then I always raise this question: suppose I lost what I have—my life, my health, my family, my home, my job, my happiness, my freedom, my peace, my serenity. How terrible it would be! Well, if this is so, then let me rejoice exultantly right away at possessing all these riches. . . .

I was barely installed in my prison when a new victim was thrown into the cell next to mine. It was Bernard, the *passeur!* We could talk to each other from cell to cell. He told me that he had gone to the families of the people he had helped cross the border to give them the good news and collect the second half of his reward. When he arrived at the apartment of the young man whose suitcase I had carried, a gentleman opened the door, asked him to step in and inquired about the fate of his nephew. He then went to the next room to get the money and returned with a group of Gestapo men, who arrested him.

We agreed on several details regarding our answers during interrogation. He was the first one to be called upstairs. The Gestapo did not seem to care much about my friend and me.

Several days passed. Prison life became almost a routine: in the morning we took our blankets out to air and one of us had to carry the bucket of excrement and urine outside. We hung the blankets on ropes in the courtyard, washed our faces at a faucet and were allowed to walk around in circles to get some exercise and fresh air. The courtyard was separated from two adjoining apartment buildings by walls which could be climbed by an agile man. Bernard had assessed the situation the same way as I had and he asked me for a favor:

"Tomorrow morning could you volunteer to take the toilet bucket from your cell and stumble over it in the courtyard to create a diversion?"

His position was much graver than ours and I agreed readily. The following morning I did what he had suggested. The German guards were furious when the excrement spilled over the courtyard. I saw Bernard detach himself from his group of cell mates, who were about to reenter the prison. He disappeared behind hanging blankets which acted as a kind of screen. I learned later that he was able to climb the wall, that he jumped through a glass roof, frightened an old lady tenant, and escaped successfully from the Germans.

After about a week, L. and I were interrogated separately by a Gestapo man. He was not particularly tough with us. We told him in the minutest detail that we wanted to spend a couple of weeks in Paris and did not intend to avoid the German army. We produced all the proofs we had prearranged: our registration for the next semester at Heidelberg University, our savings accounts, etc. He simply did his job, recorded what we said, interrogated us several times during the following days to check whether we contradicted ourselves, but did not really challenge us with any vehemence or animosity.

A couple of weeks later we were transferred to another prison, the former seminary for priests of the Archdiocese of Metz, an old, stern building with large, austere rooms. My friend and I shared the same cell. Two beds and benches constituted the furniture. We had a good view of the gardens through large barred windows on an upper floor of the building. It was a real paradise compared with the Gestapo prison. Each morning we had to go through the same classical prison routine: take our blankets, shake them in the courtyard and walk around in circles. We were infested with big, gray lice. Their daily hunt and count became one of our favorite pastimes and sources of jokes.

Our imprisonment in the Grand Seminaire went on for days and we were left totally in ignorance of our fate. This was probably one of the hardest things we had to endure. I believe we would have received with relief the news that we had been condemned to six months or a year of prison. It was the uncertainty of our fate which was hard to take. Then, one morning, as we were speculating once more about our future, a German guard entered our room and told us without any explanation that we were free to go!

My friend hastened to his home in town and I rushed to the nearby railroad station, where I had one of the most intense pleasures of my life: gulping down an enormous glass of ice-cold Alsatian beer!

There was no train until evening for my hometown. I therefore remained in Metz for the afternoon and visited my uncle, the baker in the Rue des Allemands, who had gone through agony during our arrest, knowing that he would be arrested himself if it became known that he had procured the *passeur* and had hidden us in his house. We had told the Gestapo during interrogation that we had been hanging around the railroad station in Metz, talking to other young people and drinking beer with them until we obtained the name of a *passeur*.

In the afternoon I was walking in the Rue Serpenoise, the main street of Metz, enjoying my regained freedom, when suddenly I recognized someone who had just passed me: it was the young man whose suitcase I had helped carry while crossing the border! I turned around and followed him quickly to try to talk to him, but he hastened his pace, went around a corner and disappeared in the doorway of an old apartment building. I thought to myself that he either lived there and everything was all right or he did not, and he would come out after a while. I kept watch and after a lapse of time, probably feeling reassured that I had not followed him, he reemerged right next to me! I grabbed him by the collar and asked him:

"Look, what is going on? I have the impression that you recognized me and that you are trying to avoid me. I was released from prison today. What happened to you? Let us go and have a beer. I want to hear your explanation of why you are here and not on the other side of the border, in France."

He accompanied me; we sat down in a nearby pub and ordered two beers. He then told me the following story:

"As a young boy I was sent to France from Germany, in the 1930s. My parents were refugees, but the real reason for their settling in France was to raise me as a full Frenchman so that later I could serve as a German agent. When Germany invaded France I entered the espionage service and I was assigned here to Alsace-Lorraine. In the instance which is known to you, I turned for help to the *passeur* as if I were a young Lorrainer wanting to escape from German military service. I took the last place in your column and was making signals behind my back to the German patrols with a flashlight. But these fools did not see anything. After we crossed the border I left you, returned to Metz and had you arrested, for I knew your exact location. My main objective was to capture the *passeur*. We got him later in a trap we set for him in Metz. I know that you and your friend were not trying to escape from the German draft because you told me so at a moment when you had no reason for lying. I reported that to my colleagues of the Gestapo, and I am glad to see that you were released."

The strange thing is that he had all the appearance of a really nice young man. He looked French, and not Nazi at all. He had an appealing smile and a very good-natured face. This was probably due to his French education. I told him that I had no hard feelings against him, paid for the beers, said good-bye and turned another page of my life.

As I write this story many years later, it strikes me as a good example of the long-term implantation of spies which is resorted to by many national intelligence services. As a matter of fact, not long ago, the world learned with astonishment that one of Chancellor Willy Brandt's closest collaborators had been sent as a refugee from East to West Germany years ago, in a way very similar to that of my Gestapo informant. When Chancellor Brandt visited Secretary-General U Thant at the United Nations in 1971, that spy was sitting across the table from me in the Secretary-General's conference room on the thirty-eighth floor of the United Nations! The decision of the X. family (see the chapter "The German Spy," page 88) to stay in my grandfather's village and to acquire French nationality after World War I may very well have been planned by the Germans in a similar way.

13

Getting Rid of a Draft to the German Army

Always believe that self-induced optimism and a positive attitude can do miracles even in the worst circumstances of life.

The end of September 1943. I was staying at my parents' home, trying to figure out what I could do next. My father insisted that I should try again to cross the border, but this was becoming increasingly difficult, well nigh impossible. Paid crossings with the help of professional *passeurs* were extremely risky as I had just learned at my own expense. I could not afford to resort again to this hazardous way.

The thought occurred to my father to have recourse to a friend whom my grandfather had helped in similar circumstances in 1918 and who now held a very high position in the German administration in Lorraine. I was to pay him a visit at his castle situated in the valley of the Moselle on the new border between Germany and France. But things turned out differently, for when I talked about my project to Marguerite Tonnellier, an aunt of mine who lived in the village of Ancy-sur-Moselle, not far from the castle, she felt that my father's friend was much too committed to the Nazis to be trusted in such a delicate affair. I visited the castle but did not talk to the man about my project. In the meantime my aunt arranged my escape with the help of friends who were railroad workers and who lived across the border in France. I was to be picked up by a train engine at midnight in a week's time on the main line between Metz and Paris near the border. My aunt's friends needed some time to plan the escape and to arrange the details. This plan seemed to be quite feasible as it was a private arrangement involving no more than two or three persons.

When I returned home to deliver this good news, I found my family waiting for me with grim faces. My father handed me a blue sheet of paper. It was a *Stellungsbefehl*, an order to join the German army in four days. I sat down, reflected intensely for a while, remembered the good advice of Dr. Coué, according to which a self-induced optimistic and positive attitude can do miracles in the worst circumstances of life,[1] and I said to my father:

"Do you still have a bottle of French champagne left from prewar?"

"Yes, why? You do not mean to celebrate your induction to the Nazi army, I presume?"

"Of course not. What I mean is that I will get rid of that draft notice, and I want you to prepare a bottle of champagne to celebrate my success."

"You are crazy. How can you do that?"

"Leave it to me. I have a plan which has got to work. As a matter of fact, there is no reason to panic."

And I told him the outcome of my visit to Ancy-sur-Moselle. I needed more time, however, and it was absolutely essential to get rid of the order. It was Thursday and I was to leave for the German army on Monday morning.

I left the house and went to the Kommandantur, which was swarming with draftees. I asked to talk to the officer who had issued my draft notice. He received me and I told

---

[1] See "Thank you, Dr. Coué," in *Most of All, They Taught Me Happiness.*

him of my utter astonishment at having been given an order to join the German army just a few weeks before my final examinations at the University of Heidelberg. I used my preferred line with the Nazis:

"You come here to Alsace-Lorraine, heralding all over the rooftops how different you are and how well you will run the country. What will a young man like me think of people who are so badly organized that they send him a draft notice a few weeks before his final examinations? I have killed myself to prepare for those tests and to finish my academic studies before being drafted. Do you expect me to start all over again after the war? I do not call this orderly administration. It is mismanagement of the highest degree, and if you continue on the same course you will alienate the population of this entire region."

He was angry at me for my remarks, but he could not care less and said that I had only to blame myself for not having informed his office of my forthcoming examinations. The only man who could help me in the circumstances was the head of the Kommandantur.

I had to wait for a while until the latter received me. He was an enormous, jolly, affable man in his late fifties who asked me to sit down and had a nice chat with me. He was a lawyer in civilian life and had studied in Heidelberg, where he still knew a few professors. We exchanged views on some of them. I explained my situation to him and he said he could consider withdrawing the draft notice only upon presentation of a certificate from the university informing him of my impending examinations.

I had been hoping for that and said:

"Today is Thursday and I am to leave on Monday. I will never receive such a paper in time from Heidelberg."

After a moment of reflection I asked:

"Would it do if I requested that information by telegram?"

"All right," he said, "provided they confirm it later in writing."

I thanked him, rushed home and studied the railroad timetable. I needed to reach Heidelberg the same day, send off a cable from there the following morning, be back home around midday, receive the telegram and bring it to the Kommandantur before the closing office hour. The only way to accomplish this was to ride by bicycle to Saarbrücken, leave my bike there and take a fast train to Heidelberg via Frankfurt.

I equipped myself with all the official university papers I could find and arrived in Heidelberg in the evening as scheduled. The following morning I paid a visit to the university office and while a secretary had her back turned, I stole a blank sheet of paper with the university's letterhead. Back at the hotel, I asked for the use of a typewriter and wrote a certificate whereby Professor Walter Thoms, Dean of the Faculty of Economics, authorized me to send an official telegram on his behalf. With a potato cut in half,[2] I transferred on it the best official university seal I could find among my papers. Then I went to the post office and addressed the following telegram to myself:

"At your request, I confirm that you have fulfilled all requirements to present yourself for the final examinations for the master's degree in October. Letter follows. Heil Hitler. Walter Thoms, Dean."

I went to the men's room to transfer with my potato yet another seal on that telegram and I took it to the counter. It was accepted without any questions.

I rushed to the station, took the train back to Saar-

2. Certain seals were hand printed with an ink which permitted their transfer onto another paper by means of a potato freshly cut in half. This method was widely used during the German occupation to make false certificates.

brücken, rode fifteen kilometers on my bicycle and arrived home exhausted, especially after climbing the long and very steep hill leading from the center of the town to our house. I asked my father anxiously:

"Did a telegram arrive for me?"

"What telegram? We did not receive anything. The postman has passed already and he had nothing for you. What have you been doing in Heidelberg? How are things going?"

At that point, I was rather close to giving up hope. Many precious hours had passed. Perhaps the telegram would not arrive in time and all my efforts would have been vain. After all, a war was going on and one could not expect telegraphic services to be perfect.

But luck was on my side. The telegram arrived later in the afternoon, and I ran with it to the Kommandantur just before closing time. The jolly commandant gave the necessary instructions and the *Stellungsbefehl* was withdrawn in exchange for a postponement certificate for the end of October. I left the Kommandantur, dashed home, triumphantly exhibited the pink slip of paper before the eyes of my astonished father and asked him to open his bottle of champagne. I lifted my glass to my good compatriot, Dr. Coué, who had taught me never to give up hope and to believe in one's success in almost any circumstance of life.

After the war, my father told me that when my ruse was discovered, the Kommandantur hushed it up: they were afraid of being ordered to the Russian front if higher authorities learned how easily they could be duped. Needless to say, in order to obtain the master's degree, I would have had to wait for another full year, and Walter Thoms, the most notorious Nazi of the University of Heidelberg, was certainly the last man on earth who would have helped any student, especially an Alsace-Lorrainer, to obtain a postponement from the honor of serving the *grossdeutsche Armee!*

Well, together with my escape from the Gestapo men who were on the verge of arresting me,[3] this is probably the war anecdote of which I am proudest. Many people would not have tried to do what I did and would have given up. But I was so much under the beneficial influence of Dr. Coué's philosophy that this was for me the natural way to act. Is there a sickness? Deny it, give confidence to the trillions of little cells of your body, reestablish their healthy, normal, harmonious functioning, switch on the positive buttons on your brain's central command board, those marked optimism, confidence, positive thinking. Devise the right program for your immensely capable being to pass around or conquer any obstacles placed in your way by circumstances or by other human beings. Be the best navigator there is on a stormy ocean of events and human actions. As a matter of fact, later on I was to apply this philosophy to my entire life and in particular to my work in the United Nations. Sometimes young people whom I train ask me this question: "How can you remain optimistic in a UN so full of obstacles, surrounded by so much incomprehension and enmity and faced with the most impossible problems on earth? How do you not lose hope in a world dominated by petty interests and bureaucracy.

I answer: "Please never come up again with this easy excuse. Even if you could prove to me that 39,999 of the world's 40,000 international servants are petty bureaucrats —which is by far not the case—I would not change my course by an inch. I have no power over the behavior of others, but I have absolute power and freedom over myself.

[3] See Thank you, Dr. Coué, in *Most of All, They Taught Me Happiness.*

Therefore, even if the whole world would think and act differently, I would not change my mind and attitude."

This is a rather inelegant, down-to-earth way of putting it, for I have never had the time to become a great writer or philosopher, but I can adduce two texts from famous authors whom I applaud with all my heart (in both texts the word man should be replaced by human):

> Of all paths a man could strike into, there is, at any given moment, a best path for every man; a thing which, here and now, it were of all things wisest for him to do; which could he but be led or driven to do, he were then doing "like a man," as we phrase it. His success, in such case, were complete, his felicity a maximum. This path, to find this path, and walk in it, is the one thing needful for him.
>
> *Carlyle*

> Every man has his own vocation. There is one direction in which all space is open to him. He has faculties silently inviting him thither to endless exertion. He is like a ship in a river; he runs against obstructions on every side but one; on that side all obstruction is taken away, and he sweeps serenely over a deepening channel into an infinite sea.
>
> *Emerson*

14

The German Spy

The only sensible, worthwhile objective on this planet is to work for the peace, cooperation and well-being of all peoples.

When Alsace-Lorraine became French in 1919, after World War I, certain criteria were established for the acquisition of French nationality. Persons whose parents were both born in Alsace-Lorraine automatically became French. Those who had one German parent had to apply for French citizenship and were given it only after investigation of their behavior during the German time.

In the village of my grandfather, Sarralbe, lived a family X., whose father was German. As a hat manufacturer and a member of the municipal council, my grandfather was one of the local notables. X. turned to him for help in acquiring French nationality. My grandfather vouched for him, for he knew the family well and regarded X. as a fine gentleman.

When I was a child I often heard my father speak about the son of X., who had gone to the same local school, had pursued his studies in college and had become an officer in the French army. My father mistrusted him thoroughly. Whenever he saw him during his visits in our town, he looked worried all day and once I heard him say:

"X. the father may have been a fine gentleman, but as for his son, if I were the French, I would not trust him for a

moment. His heart is definitely German and he does not fit
into a French officer's uniform."

Then came World War II, the evacuation of the borderland, the defeat of France and the return of the people of
Alsace-Lorraine to their plundered or demolished homes.

We were busy like everybody else putting our house in
order. It had served successively as an artillery observation
post for the French troops and later as quarters for German
infantrymen who were still there when we came home.
One day, in June 1940, a powerful German limousine
stopped in front of the house and out of it popped a German
official wearing the uniform of a high-ranking Nazi digni-
tary.

It was the son of X.![1] He avowed to my father that his
family had a great debt of gratitude toward the Mullers,
since my grandfather had vouched for them, thus allowing
him to become French and to serve as a German spy in the
French army during all these years! He gave several examples of the carelessness of the French. The Germans apparently possessed the plans of the entire Maginot Line. Some
of the French equipment in the underground fortress had
even been manufactured in Germany! He said to my father:

"I am now a very powerful man in Lorraine. The Führer has appointed me deputy Gauleiter of the province. I
will be residing in Metz and in a nearby country castle. I
know what I owe your family. If there is anything I can do
for you, please do not hesitate to ask me. I will do everything I can."

My father mumbled:

"One thing the Germans could do is to help me get
back my hat-making machinery, which has been evacuated
to Metz."

---

[1] For the sake of simplicity I will call him X. henceforth.

X. gave orders and a few days later the machines were delivered to our home, to the great joy of my father since hat making was his entire life.

We never saw X. again. He was too busy helping the Germans annex Alsace-Lorraine without waiting for a peace treaty with France.

Three years passed. Young men from our region were being enlisted in the German army despite the protests of Marshal Pétain. My first attempt to cross the border to France had failed. A second failure would mean deportation of my family to Poland and my dispatch in a disciplinary regiment to the Russian front. What could I do? My father continued to insist that I should flee to France despite the risks involved for the family. But we knew no one who could help me or whom we could trust.

As I mentioned in the preceding anecdote regarding my trip to Ancy-sur-Moselle, my father said to me:

"Look, perhaps the time has come to turn to X. for help. He is living in his castle near Metz, on the border with France. Go and see him. All he can do is to refuse. He will not have you arrested."

I obeyed and traveled to the little village of Ancy-sur-Moselle, in the valley of the Moselle, not far from X.'s castle. In that village lived my aunt Marguerite Tonnellier, the sister of one of my uncles through marriage. She was a widow and made a modest living from growing strawberries and delicious yellow plums called mirabelles, the raw material for a famous Lorraine brandy bearing the same name. From there I could easily walk or ride by bicycle to X.'s castle. I took lodging at my aunt's place and told her that I was going to visit X.

She could not believe her ears and exclaimed:

"In God's name, why should you want to see that Boche? He is the worse Nazi on earth, and you are telling me that you want to pay him a visit? For what reason, may I ask?"

I told her of my quandary and my father's decision to send me to X. for help. She snapped back:

"You are a fool and your father too. I would not trust this Boche for a second. I beg you not to go. He will have you arrested."

I resolved nevertheless to go, but promised her that I would wait until the very last moment before talking to him about my problem.

On my way to the castle, I was stopped several times by German policemen and field gendarmes, for the road followed the French border very closely. But when they heard that I was going to visit X., they clicked their heels and saluted me with loud Heil Hitlers.

I finally reached the castle and was led by an aide to a vast waiting room adorned with magnificent antique tapestries. A big party was going on next door. I peeked through the curtains: several dozen German officers and Nazi officials were celebrating and drinking champagne. After a while X. came to see me and I introduced myself as the son of Muller, the hat maker. In my mind I had already decided that I would not confide in this man. He might very well help me cross the border, but on the other side he would have me arrested under conditions which would not allow my father to suspect his treason. I told him therefore simply that I was spending my vacation with my aunt in a neighboring village and that my father had asked me to go and say hello to him. He inquired about my family and my studies, offered me a cup of champagne and I took leave, sickened by the Nazi atmosphere which reigned in that castle.

My aunt was delighted to learn that I had not asked him for help. In the meantime she had talked to a friend of hers in the village who had family on the other side of the border, and it was with their assistance that I successfully crossed the border sometime later.

This was not the end of the story. History continued to sweep its waves over Alsace-Lorraine, as it had done for centuries, in ever-widening circles finally embracing the entire world.

During the winter offensive of 1944, most of Alsace-Lorraine was liberated, including my hometown Sarreguemines, where the front stabilized along the river Saar. One day, the brother-in-law of X., a local merchant, came to see my father:

"X. is in town. He is fleeing from the Allies. He needs a safe place to hide for a few days until things have calmed down. My own house is not safe because our relations with him are known. Your father helped his family after World War I. He sends me to ask you if you could help him again."

"The hell with him," said my father. "We suffered enough from the Germans and my only regret is that my father was foolish enough to vouch for his family in 1919. Tell him he should be happy that I do not report him immediately to the French or American police."

The brother-in-law left furious and for some time my parents did not hear anything about X.'s fate.

A few months later, however, the local merchant told my father triumphantly that X. was out of danger and that he was now working for the Americans as a spy![2] The Americans must, however, have gotten wise to him, for soon thereafter we learned that X. had moved to the capital of a Latin American country where he represented a large German industrial firm!

---

[2] This was reminiscent of the famous Barbie case.

This was still not the end of the story. On one of my home leaves to France after I joined the United Nations, my father greeted me with this news:

"Do you know that the grandson of the X. family, namely the son of X., who must be about your age, is working for the United Nations? His uncle, the local merchant, was all too happy to brag about it, since this puts our two families on a par."

I was startled. The real name of the X. family was not a common one and I had never heard it mentioned at the UN. When I returned to New York, I consulted the list of UN personnel at headquarters and, as I expected, could not find his name. But my father kept insisting that he held an important position at the UN.

Many years passed. My good parents died and I forgot all about the X. family. Then, one day, while I was working as an aide to Secretary-General U Thant, trouble broke out in an Asian country and I received a telegram reporting on the local situation and asking for instructions from the Secretary-General regarding the evacuation of UN personnel. The cable was labeled: "To Muller from X."! I later sent him back a cable, "From Muller to X.", conveying the views and instructions of the Secretary-General. X. Junior, so I discovered, was indeed an official of one of the UN programs! I had simply never met him or heard about him because he had always worked in the field while I myself had remained at UN headquarters.

I held his cable in my hands for a long while. History once more had widened its circles. What strange vagaries our lives had seen! I have never met X. Junior to this day, but if I should meet him, I would tell him how happy I was that the two sons of our fathers and grandsons of our grandfathers, from our poor war-torn borderland of Alsace-Lorraine, were at long last working for the only sensible, worthwhile objective on this planet, namely the peace, cooperation and well-being of all peoples. Our fate could be taken as a living testimony of the progress accomplished by humanity since World War II.

We should indeed both be happy and grateful that one of the positive effects of World War II was the creation of a universal organization which gave young people like us the opportunity of constructive, positive lives. Whenever I see young people working for the UN, UNICEF, the UN Development Programme, the UN Volunteers, the World Health Organization or any other of the UN's thirty-two specialized programs and agencies, I feel an immense leap of joy and gratitude in my heart for all those—governments, taxpayers, philanthropists, UNICEF volunteers and gift shops —to whose contributions these young people owe their meaningful lives. Ours is no longer a world in which young people must dream of becoming soldiers or spies, but where their ideal can be to work for peace, justice and the greatest happiness for the largest number of people on this planet. The son of X. the spy and the son of the hat maker thank you all for our beautiful lives which you have made possible. And I hope that someday infinitely more will be done and that my proposal for a world peace service will be accepted, replacing military service in many countries of the world.[3]

[3.] The proposal has been worked out by the University for Peace in Costa Rica.

15

On a Train Engine

We should pause as pilgrims at those places on earth where our hearts have beaten a little stronger in joy or in fear.

My aunt Marguerite Tonnellier in Ancy-sur-Moselle had a close friend, Yvonne Antoine, whose brothers were railroad workers and lived in the village of Pagny-sur-Moselle on the other side of the border. Between Pagny and Ancy the little station of Novéant had become an important railway traffic center, since all trains between Paris and Germany via Metz and Saarbrücken had to pass military and customs controls at that point. The two Antoine brothers were locomotive engineers and usually worked together on the same shift in Novéant. (These were the friends with whom my aunt Marguerite had made arrangements for my escape.)

I had to be ready on a Wednesday at midnight, just a few days after I had gotten rid of the order to join the German army. When the day came, the two women dressed me as a railroad worker: black shirt and black pants, black cap, an oil lamp and a long hammer. They also darkened my face with candle soot. I took off my glasses, which made me look too much like an intellectual. At eleven o'clock in the evening we walked down from the village to the railway tracks, which followed the Moselle River. At a specified signal post outside of Novéant, we hid in a trench and waited for the arrival of the engine run by the Antoine brothers.

The hour that elapsed until midnight had a strange, unforgettable quality: it was a mixture of peace and anxiety, of silence and sounds. Nature was at rest and the night was silent, and yet there was an intensive invisible life in the high grasses and in the ground. Our bodies were still, and yet we could hear the beatings of our hearts. The villagers were asleep, but we could hear trains whistle and authoritarian Germans shout orders in the railroad station, trying to accelerate Hitler's conquest of the world. Tucked together, we alternately whispered, chuckled or froze at the slightest sound. But nobody was around at this late hour.

At long last we saw a locomotive move in our direction and stop exactly at the height of the signal post. A man waved a lantern as is customary during engine maneuvers at night. In this case it meant that it was the engine operated by the Antoine brothers. I kissed the two women good-bye, ran toward the engine and climbed on board. Two dirty, blackened engineers briefly greeted me and swiftly drove the locomotive back into the station. There they maneuvered around until the engine was fastened to a freight train which had just been inspected by the German police and customs. Uniformed Germans were swarming all over the place, checking doors and seals, shouting orders and filling out papers, but none of them paid any attention to the engine. The two brothers smiled at me and gave me to understand that everything would be all right.

The train then took off and puffed and huffed toward France. At the very moment when we crossed the border, the two brothers blew the whistle triumphantly, pulled out a bottle of schnapps, offered me a gulp and broke out into a cheerful laughter. In Pagny, we left the engine and walked to their father's home, where a hearty meal awaited us. After a few days with the Antoine family, I was put on a freight train going to a little town in the north of France, Chauny, where an uncle of mine, Alphonse Schaeffer, harbored me until I could cross the border into southern unoccupied France.

How many times since then, when returning from the United States to Alsace-Lorraine and traveling from Paris to Metz, have I passed through the little stations of Pagny, Novéant and Ancy! The train rushes through them like lightning today and pays them no attention. But behind a window stands a man who tries to catch a glimpse of the spot where many years ago, not far from the imposing ruins of a Roman aqueduct crossing the Moselle River, he had waited in the night for a railroad engine, accompanied by two young and courageous women. And life goes on with the lightning speed of that train in this vast world of ours where there is so little time to pay homage to our past and to pause as pilgrims at those places where our heart has beaten a little more strongly, in joy or in fear.

16

The Supreme Test

*Prayer has the strength of giving us the vision
of another world, a better world, the world we
dream of.*

The rest of my wartime adventures would occupy a full
volume, which I hope to write someday, but I wish to high-
light here one or two more stories which were particularly
instructive from the human point of view or which had a
certain historical value. The first story has to deal with the
fear of death. I have often wondered what I would feel in
case of impending death. Some people have actually written down their impressions in this regard, but most others
rapidly turn away from the dreadful thought, for humans
love to close their eyes to death, as if they were immortal.
Every person also clings to some hope until the very end,
thus proving that humans are not born for pessimism and
destruction but for the defense and assertion of life. If nothing else helps, the last words are usually "mother" or
"God," a call to the origin of life itself, a deep and instinctive
perception of the eternal trilogy of life, death and resurrection.

Perhaps the supreme test comes when a man, in full,
conscious possession of his faculties and awareness, is about
to die under the bullets of a firing squad. I had the sad
experience of witnessing several executions during the last
year of the war. Knowing that the same could very well

happen to me if the Nazis caught me, I tried to place myself in the situation of the condemned person, in order to be prepared and to learn as much as possible from the frightful experience. And there was definitely something to learn, as I will try to show in the following story.

After my narrow escape from arrest by the Gestapo in Vichy (see "Thank You, Dr. Coué" in *Most of All, They Taught Me Happiness*), thanks to another member of my family, my uncle Maurice Tonnellier, I joined an active Maquis in the hills of Auvergne in the valley of the upper Loire. Our headquarters were located in a small village—La Chapelle—on top of a hill from which one commanded a remarkable circular view over all possible approaches by the Germans. Upon my arrival, I was subjected to intensive military training, and I did not participate at first in any active operations. These were carried out by experienced Maquisards who had definite targets, using very daring methods at considerable risk. Some of them were caught, tortured and killed, others came back with weapons, money or prisoners. One of the first gruesome stories I heard upon my arrival was that of a young man who had been carrying a message on motorcycle and was found later tied with barbed wire to a tree, shot and horribly mutilated.

Later on, I was assigned to a group of nine Russians who had escaped from the garrison of St. Etienne, where they had been held semi-prisoners by the Germans. The Nazis let Russian prisoners practically die of hunger and then offered them the opportunity to join the Vlassov army, which collaborated with them. They were given German uniforms and were paraded through the cities of occupied territories to give the impression that there were still important German troops left. These nine Russians were highly trained soldiers and I am sure I owe my life to their experience and skill. We communicated with each other in

German and later on in broken Russian, after I had learned some of their language.

One day, three members of our Maquis returned to the village with a notable prisoner: an informer of the French Milice—a special police force which collaborated with the Nazis against their own compatriots. The Maquisards had driven a black Citroën—the customary wartime French official car—to the outskirts of the city of St. Etienne where, at the house of friends, they dressed in the dark blue uniforms of the Milice and affixed on their vehicle the insignia of the French special police. Knowing the habits of the man they wanted to capture, they waited for him near the headquarters of the Milice. When he showed up, they drove speedily toward him and asked him to hop into the car in order to accompany them to a spot outside the town where a massive arrest of members of the underground was supposedly taking place. Until they were in safe territory, the Maquisards acted as if they were members of the Milice. Then they drew their guns, disarmed the man and brought him to our village where he was kept prisoner in the schoolhouse and subjected to interrogation. I had had a glimpse of him when he arrived: he was a stocky, strong-featured, ruddy man in his forties who resembled innumerable other Frenchmen of his age. I did not witness any of the interrogations, but we all knew what was happening and that the classical torture of the *baignoire,* or bathtub, was applied to him. Hands tied behind his back, the prisoner's head was plunged into a basin of water and held there until near-suffocation. This was repeated until the victim confessed everything he knew. We learned that the prisoner was extremely courageous and that it took many *baignoires* and a lot of beating to make him talk. On the morning of the third day, the rumor spread that he was going to be shot. An offer to the Germans to exchange him for one of our comrades had been rejected. I was assigned to the group which led

him to the execution ground. I saw him emerge from the
schoolhouse, bearing hardly any resemblance to the man he
had been on his arrival: his face was red, blue and green,
except for a few livid spots where by some miracle he had
not been hit; his eyes and lips were atrociously tumefied; his
shirt and pants were all wet and in shreds.

Hands tied behind his back, he started to walk rather
proudly and erect on the road to death, as if wanting to
prove to the onlooking villagers and Maquisards his
strength and dignity. For a good part of the route he be-
haved in the same impressive manner. Then, all of a sudden, halfway, he stopped abruptly and a total change overcame him. The image of death must have struck him like a
flash and the strength that had held him together broke
down utterly. He refused to advance, started to shiver, to
cry, to plead and to beg, and threw himself on the ground.
He refused to stand up, collapsed time and again when we
tried to hold him up, and finally had to be dragged by his
feet to the place of execution. It was one of the most pitiful
scenes I have witnessed in my life. Unable to use his hands
and feet, he was desperately biting the ground and every
bunch of grass on his way, as if he could thereby retard the
fatal moment. One of his front teeth broke off. I saw it
glimmer for a while in the dust of the road. Through his
pants, wet excrement began to appear. His blood-covered
face was almost inhuman when we arrived at the wood.
There, a grave had been dug in a clearing. He refused to
stand up. Kneeling on the ground, holding his head down
between his legs to avoid the bullets, he was sobbing like a
child, totally impervious to the exhortations of our officer at
least to die like a man. I wondered whether the firing squad
would be ordered to shoot into this miserable bundle of
wounded flesh. But suddenly, with astonishing alacrity, he
jumped to his feet and shouted from his lacerated face:

"Vive le Maquis! Sauvez-moi!" (Hail the Maquis! Save me!)

At that precise moment the salvo of guns cracked and knocked him into his grave.

I felt sick for long moments afterward and tried to relive time and again the physical and mental agonies of this poor, wretched being. I could well understand his attitude of despair, hope and terror, but I felt that this was definitely not the way to die.

As the war drew to a close, the Germans grew weaker in France, and the operations of the Maquis became more intensive. General Koenig, our commander in London, ordered the Maquis to pursue, capture and destroy as many Germans as possible and prevent their return and regrouping in Germany. More weapons and demolition experts were parachuted to us to help us blow up railroad tracks, bridges, tunnels and waterways. Finally, in July of 1944, after French and American forces had landed in the south of France, the Germans began to leave our region and to evacuate their troops back to Germany. One day we learned that the entire garrison from the city of Le Puy was moving through the hills to join the main route of escape: the Rhone Valley. In an operation known as the battle of Estivareilles, we captured the entire column, a total of six hundred Germans. Among them were a dozen French collaborators who were trying to escape to Germany in fear of reprisals by the local population. The German soldiers and officers were kept prisoners in La Chapelle and remained unharmed.

But it was a different matter with the French traitors. Our commander set up an extraordinary tribunal to pass judgment on them. From Le Puy came testimonies and information about their nefarious activities. Half of them were condemned to death, and the others were sent back to

Le Puy to be tried there. Once more my unit had to escort the condemned to the execution ground.

People in a group act differently in the face of death: the weak are impressed by the strong and dare less to give vent to their fears. At no time did the group show any signs of panic or breakdown. All acted in a dignified communion of fate. There was a woman among them, a very beautiful and sweet-looking creature. She must have caused a lot of harm to the Maquis to be shot, for the other two women in the group of collaborators had been spared. Contrary to the ugly custom of shaving the heads of such girls naked and painting a *Hakenkreuz* on them, her hair had been untouched and she had not suffered any bodily violence. She was a full, healthy human being at the height of her youth and beauty. I wondered what thoughts and images could occupy her mind on the road to death. She walked silently, looking at no one and keeping her eyes fixed on the ground. Her lips were imperceptibly moving: she was praying. Having arrived at the freshly dug graves, the men stood erect and she knelt in front of hers, facing the firing squad. Then she started to pray loudly, with great fervor and a crystal-clear voice, and peace reigning on her face. She was reciting the Hail Mary in Latin. The metallic sounds of the rifles being readied mingled with the ancient Roman words in the silent wood. The condemned men shouted a loud *"Vive la France."* The shots knelled, cutting the prayer of the woman in two, and I saw her body flip over, as if struck by a violent blow, into her grave. . . . Human beings in the flower of their age had left this world for all eternity. But they had died with dignity, the men clinging to their belief that they had acted for the good of their country and the woman having resorted to prayer. Her example impressed me most. I could visualize her feelings, her peace and her oblivion of the life she was quitting. Prayer has the strength of giving one the vision of another world, a better world, the world above, the world beyond, the world we all dream of, a world of peace and decency, and this must have helped her enormously to triumph over her fear of death. Should I ever face a similar fate, I would certainly follow her example. Deeply moved by her stoicism, I received in my heart her poor Ave Maria cut in pieces by the bullets and finished it as her last homage to heaven and to God.

Twenty years later, during the summer of 1964, I was driving with my family from Spain to Geneva, where I was stationed with the European Office of the United Nations. In the south of France we ran into some terrible traffic snags. Miles of cars were piling up each time the main road crossed one of the medieval French cities around which no peripheral roads had as yet been built. It was a nightmare under the hot summer sun. I studied the map to see whether there was another way to reach Geneva and found a series of winding, secondary roads leading through the hills of Auvergne. That route would take us longer, but it might be instructive for my children to visit the places of my underground time. I was curious myself to see what had become of them after so many years. My suggestion to change route was adopted, and soon we found ourselves on the rocky, desolate plateau of south-central France. After a long journey we reached Le Puy, the cultural capital of Auvergne, a fascinating city erected in the crater of an extinguished volcano at the center of which, on a rocky needle, is perched a famous chapel. I had never been in Le Puy and we had great pleasure in visiting the old city, built with volcanic rocks, known for its cathedral, its pilgrimages and its lace-making artisans. We spent the night there, and the following morning we took the same road which the retreating Germans had used twenty years ago. We reached Estivareilles, a village nestled in the upper valley of the Loire where the river is still a turbulent stream seeking its way through the hills and rocky plateau. I was able to recognize many sights, and I described with much excitement and in great detail to my family the way in which we had fought and captured the Germans. The bridge in the village was now a comfortable motorway. I told my children how we blew it up, how the Germans then built a wooden bridge during the night, and how negotiations were conducted for their surrender. At dawn, I met the first German midway on the bridge. He handed me his weapons, among which was a fine revolver he had won at a shooting contest in his city in northern Germany and which I have kept to this day in our farmhouse in France.

It seemed hard to believe that so much turmoil had reigned in this peaceful place. But a nearby monument bore witness that I was not dreaming. On it were engraved the names of several comrades, including that of Commandant Marey, who was later killed as a regular officer in North Africa.

We had a cup of coffee in the restaurant near the bridge. It was Sunday morning. Several Frenchmen dropped in for their apéritif. I talked to them, but no one remembered much about the war. They were young children at that time, and they made me feel suddenly old. Like my offspring, they were not very interested in the past. Their attention was concentrated on the pinball machines, the football game and the jukebox.

We then drove up the hill to La Chapelle. The village had barely changed. It seemed petrified in time. The inhabitants were in their homes, having their Sunday meal. The place seemed deserted, devoid of human life, but images, faces, names, scenes, movements, maneuvers, arms and parachutes began to flood my memory. A whole vanished world became alive between me and the silent village. I was scurrying from one place to another, describing to my children phantasmagoric scenes in totally empty landscapes:

here, around the village fountain, Russian soldiers were singing their wonderful folk and army songs in the evening, surrounded by the curious villagers who had never seen a Russian in their lives and who were deeply moved by their soul-shaking chants. Here in this large wooden barn we had our lodgings, each of us being entitled to a pile of hay, a potato sack for our belongings and a bundle of arms. Here in this room of the schoolhouse I had taught French to the Russians and they had taught Russian to me. In this other room on the first floor, the informer of the Milice had been tortured. Here in this room I had spent hours with other comrades counting money stolen from the rich merchants in the cities. Here in this vast open field, after an agreed signal from London radio, we lit the headlights of three cars arranged in a large triangle, and at a specified hour in the night a plane could be heard overhead, soon parachuting containers of arms to us. Here in this farmhouse our kitchen was located. I could not resist any longer: I had to talk to someone. So I knocked at the door of that farm and a man appeared who asked us to enter. I was met by the same kettle-boiled potato odor as twenty years ago. I could still see myself sitting in that kitchen, peacefully peeling potatoes.

The man told us that he had not lived there during the war. He had married into the family after the hostilities. As a result I did most of the talking and reminiscing and he mostly listened. But he suddenly remembered something and said:

"Would you like to see some of the empty American containers in which your arms were parachuted?"

He took us to the back of the house. There, in a pig stall, a series of half-containers had been welded together and were used as troughs for the animals! He pointed at the roof of an outhouse and said:

"The metal sheet you see up there is also made of flattened American containers."

I wondered at the extraordinary vagaries of life: up here in the hills of Auvergne, in the silence of a forlorn, peaceful village, twenty years after the war, American containers made in Detroit or Chicago were covering the roof of an outhouse and serving as feeders for pigs! What a wasteful and crazy world! I would never come to the end of my astonishment. Why was I to see so much in one life? . . .

When we took leave, the man whispered to me:

"People in the village say that you were bad boys and that you did a lot of killing up here at the time. One can still see the emplacement of the graves in the woods."

I could not resist. I had to visit again the macabre place. Retracing my very steps of twenty years ago, I led my family along the same unpaved dirt road which the condemned prisoners had taken. Using all the power of my memory, I proceeded almost straight to the clearing in the woods. There, under a thick layer of moss and grass, seven rectangular depressions could be seen, marking distinctly the places where the prisoners had been shot and buried. The first grave on the left was that of the Frenchman who was with the Milice, the next was that of the woman who had recited the Ave Maria. I stood there in silence, buried in my memories, while my boys, soon totally uninterested, were running around, picking blueberries. . . .

As we left the village, on the road down to Estivareilles, I noticed another monument. It had been erected on a spot where members of our Maquis had been killed by the Germans. I stopped the car, read out the names to my children and said:

"If the name Marco, which was given to me by my comrades, were engraved on this stone, none of you would be here today and enjoying the miracle of life. We must pray for these poor young men who were less fortunate than I and renew our pledge to work with all our fervor for a peaceful and lovely world."

While we were praying, my eyes caught sight of blue cornflowers, white daisies and red poppies, the three "flowers of France," waving their heads gently in a wheat field behind the monument. As I watched them, deeply sunk in meditation, the beautiful words of the Preamble of the UN Charter came to my mind. They fell like the beads of a rosary, like an Ave Maria meant for all peoples of earth, black and white, poor and rich, young and old, suffering and joyful, believers and nonbelievers, generations gone and generations to come, as if born from the senseless killings which have drenched so many battlegrounds of this world:

WE THE PEOPLES
OF THE UNITED NATIONS,
DETERMINED

> to save succeeding generations from the scourge of war, which twice in our lifetime has brought untold sorrow to humankind, and

> to reaffirm faith in fundamental human rights, in the dignity and worth of the human person, in the equal rights of men and women and of nations large and small, and

> to establish conditions under which justice and respect for the obligations arising from treaties and other sources of international law can be maintained, and

> to promote social progress and better standards of life in larger freedom,

AND FOR THESE ENDS

> to practice tolerance and live together in peace with one another as good neighbors, and

> to unite our strength to maintain international peace and security, and

> to ensure, by the acceptance of principles and the institution of methods, that armed force shall not be used, save in the common interest, and

> to employ international machinery for the promotion of the economic and social advancement of all peoples,

HAVE RESOLVED TO
COMBINE OUR EFFORTS TO
ACCOMPLISH THESE AIMS

> Accordingly, our respective Governments, through representatives assembled in the city of San Francisco, who have exhibited their full powers found to be in good and due form, have agreed to the present Charter of the United Nations and do hereby establish an international organization to be known as the United Nations. . . .

What would I have said if someone had told me at that time that I was to join the UN organization and be allowed to devote the rest of my life to peace? Four years after the battle of Estivareilles I swore the following oath at Lake Success, the provisional seat of the United Nations:

"I, Robert Muller, solemnly swear to exercise in all loyalty, discretion and conscience the functions entrusted to me as an international civil servant of the United Nations, to discharge these functions and regulate my conduct with the interest of the United Nations only in view, and not seek or accept instructions in regard to the performance of my duties from any Government or other authority external to the Organization."

The flowers of France were gently undulating in the summer breeze. My children, unconcerned with my bygone world, were nagging and needling each other, pursuing the endless chain of learning for life. I was thinking of my dead comrades, of the executed woman, of her Ave Maria, of the Frenchman of the Milice and his agony, and I was praying to God to spare our world any other wars and similar horrors. Love, reason, cooperation and prayer were the only ways out of our mad and still very primitive society.

As I write this today, I sometimes have the impression that I exaggerate the power of the human person to overcome suffering and the fear of death by autosuggestion, prayer or an iron will. I have been accused at the UN of being an incorrigible, stubborn optimist. An inside voice is now asking me this question:

"What would you have done if you had been captured, tortured and taken to the execution ground?"

Visualizing myself in that situation with all the strength of my imagination, my answer is:

"I would have tried with the last fiber of my mind to find a way of escape and if this proved impossible I would have fought fear until the very end."

"How?"

"Even with my fingernails being torn out and my head plunged into water, I would have thought that this was the most extraordinary experience a man could live. I would have observed and studied the reactions of my mind and body, the approaches of unconsciousness and death, the outer limits of pain, in order to alleviate suffering and avoid the tunnel of fear. Being taken to the execution ground, I would have seen my entire life, I would have been thankful to God for it and prayed to Him to receive me in His boundless mercy, certain that I would never cease to be part of the eternal stream of life, death and resurrection."

"All this is illusion, utter nonsense, total foolishness."

"I do not think so. An illusion which assuages fear and suffering is a very powerful reality."

17

The Liberation of Lyon

*I dream of the day when all armies of the
world will be part of a United Nations peace
force.*

August 1944. The Germans had been wiped out from the
Auvergne. After the battle of Estivareilles, our underground group was transported by trucks to the Rhone Valley, where, together with other French Maquis, our task
was to harass the retreating Germans. The United Nations[1]
troops had landed in the south of France. The French were
pursuing the Germans along the Rhone Valley, while an
American column of armored cars was pushing northward
from Cannes along the route Napoleon at the foot of the
Alps. Both forces were to converge and capture Lyon, the
third largest city of France. American planes were ma-
chine-gunning and bombarding everything they saw moving on the highway during the day. The Germans, therefore, could pursue their retreat only during the night. In the
daytime, their patrols were engaged in combat with the
French underground forces, whom they tried to push back
as far as possible from the main road in order to free it for
the night.

[1] This was the beautiful name under which the Allied troops fought at
that time. Peace will prevail on this planet only when all national armies
around this globe will become again parts of a United Nations army.

I will narrate two such engagements which took place near the town of Givors, to the southwest of Lyon, where our new headquarters were located.

With a patrol I was occupying a barren hill, separated from another hill by a small valley. The mound opposite us was wooded and from among the trees German sharpshooters were firing at us with high-precision rifles equipped with telescopes. It was a most excruciating experience to be shot at from invisible points, without being able to respond. Luckily none of us got hit. The closest shot was a bullet that made a neat little hole in my trousers.

On the flank of the hill facing us there was a large clearing. In the middle of it stood a wooden barn. Suddenly we saw a German soldier run as fast as he could from the woods toward the shack. My Russian companions wanted to open fire, but Gregory Trifonof, their Colonel, held them back. We waited patiently and saw four more Germans run successively at intervals to the refuge. Trifonof then ordered Kolia, our machine-gunner, to get ready and we waited.

After a while we saw a German dash out of the cabin and run like a rabbit toward the other side of the clearing. He was about to reach its fringe, when our machine gun crackled and mowed him down almost instantly. Four more times we saw men run out of the shack and each time Kolia repeated his feat. The incident was over. Dusk was beginning to fall over the hills. The fragrance of peach trees was mounting from the valley of the Rhone. We called headquarters over the field telephone and we were asked to return to Givors.

The second engagement took place on a side road near Givors. One morning we were notified that three truckloads of Germans had taken a road parallel to the highway, in an attempt either to escape northward or to attack the underground forces. About thirty young Frenchmen took positions in ditches near a road intersection toward which the Germans were progressing. My Russian group selected a small hill dominating the crossroad. In the valley of the Loire we had captured from the Germans a small Russian 76-mm cannon with a good deal of ammunition. We attached it to a passenger car—a Matford—and we were thus highly mobile, able to shoot a few shots from one spot and then change position very rapidly before the Germans could locate us.

We waited for a while until we saw the three reported trucks descend a hill toward the intersection. Colonel Trifonof decided to operate the cannon himself. With the second shot he hit one of the trucks. The Germans jumped off the vehicles and spread out in the fields, fired at by the young men in the ditches. After heavy shooting all three trucks were on fire, the bodies of most of the Germans were strewn on the ground and the rest of them surrendered. We went down to the intersection to inspect the bodies and see if any of them were still alive. The young Maquisards were jumping and running all over the field. Wallets, watches, gold rings and other belongings soon disappeared. I walked around sadly, horrified by the lacerated bodies, sickened by the blood and by the plundering. One of my Russian comrades threw a wallet at me, asking me to inspect it. I found in it pictures of four children, of a woman and her last letter to her husband. I sat down on the ground next to the dead body and read it. The woman gave him news of each of the children, of the village and of the neighbors. She finished her letter with a prayer to God that the war would soon end and bring him home safely. Tears were mounting to my eyes when I finished and saw the poor middle-aged man lying on the ground, his green uniform all soaked in blood around the abdomen. The soldiers we had killed did not look like fierce Aryan warriors. They were rather old wary family men anxious to return home.

My Russian comrade—Nuri Akshurin—called the "red-head"—noticed that I was pale and upset. He said to me:

"Marco, war is war. You could be dead instead of him. You must become a real soldier."

He grabbed a can of white, soft fat, which the Germans used to eat for quick energy, and, using his fingers, gulped it down in front of me. A light drizzling rain had begun to fall over the scene. The air was filled with a nauseating odor of blood. Gushes of black smoke from the burning trucks and gasoline swept over the fields into our faces. I felt like fainting. Nuri was looking sternly at me. All of a sudden he put his foot on the dead man's belly, pressed hard, made the blood gush out and continued to lick fat from his fingers while keeping his eyes riveted on me. I turned around and vomited painfully. He then left, laughing and commenting:

"Marco is not a soldier!"

The same day in the afternoon we were resting in a meadow near Givors, waiting for further orders. The weather was warm, and blue skies had returned. I had found a four-leaf clover and was dreaming of peace in a world of sunshine, beauty and kindness. The sound of bees and cicadas, and the fragrance of the flowering clover were slowly lulling me into sleep when a fighter from the Resistance arrived on a motorcycle and asked for me. He said:

"On the main road to Lyon we stopped a Red Cross car which looked suspicious to us. Three men were in it and after questioning them we found out that they were Germans. We killed them on the spot. Here are their wallets and billfolds. Since you know German, Commandant Marey wants you to go through them and see if they contain anything of interest."

I sat back on the grass and lived through the same scene as in the morning: pictures of children and wives, letters speaking of the end of the war and the impending return of the loved ones. The only difference was that these three victims had been officers. But there was nothing of interest in their papers. I was about to discard everything, when I decided to inspect the empty billfolds a last time. One of them, which I still possess today, had an inside lining. I tore it open. My fingers slipped between the cloth and the leather and emerged with a tiny, thin piece of paper, about twice the size of a matchbox. Something was written on it in gothic characters. My heart jumped when I read it. It was no less than the defense plan of the city of Lyon! Contrary to the speculations of the Allies, Lyon was not going to be defended seriously by the Germans. All that was foreseen was the stationing of a few platoons of men with a couple of antiaircraft cannons for use against tanks at the three main entrance roads to the city. This was tantamount to nothing. But all access bridges were to be blown up in order to retard the Allies' advance. The last paragraph stated that the next information would be delivered the following Thursday at noontime in front of the main church of Belfort, a city further to the north.

This text was of considerable importance. I immediately translated it into French and went to see Commandant Marey. I recommended that he communicate it as quickly as possible to the American column in the east, for in light of it they might well decide to push straight northward instead of converging toward Lyon. I also offered to go to Belfort and receive the next information from the Germans:

"I look like a German, I speak German perfectly, there will be no difficulty whatsoever."

But he refused, arguing that the death of the three German officers would not remain unnoticed and that it would be suicide for me to go.

At dusk, when we returned to our headquarters in Givors, we discovered that the First French Army had just arrived, to the great joy of the population. We admired their tanks and arms, compared with which the weaponry parachuted to us looked very poor indeed.

Suddenly word spread through town that there had been a severe dispute between Commandant Marey and the commander of the regular troops. The latter had established his headquarters in city hall. Marey had gone to see him and had given him the information about the sparse defenses of Lyon and the planned blowing up of all the bridges. Marey begged him to continue his advance and to capture Lyon the same evening, thus saving France several vital bridges and billions of francs. But the commander of the regulars refused. He had received orders to spend the night in Givors. Marey, who was accustomed to more freedom of action, shouted at him, asked him to get new orders and, when he failed, apparently got into a fight with him. He wanted to proceed himself to Lyon, but soon thereafter received orders from higher up to submit to the French commander. His freedom as an underground fighter had come to an end.

I never saw such a wild and desperate man. Tiny, wiry, jumping to decisions with lightning speed, he had come to the last act of his incredible career. I asked him for permission to let me go to Lyon with Colonel Trifonof in our small covered truck in which we had installed a loudspeaker to exhort Germans, Russians and Poles to surrender. This technique had proved very successful in the Auvergne and I wanted to proceed with my own adventure while the rest of our group was stranded in Givors. He shrugged his shoulders, totally uninterested, and said:

"Do what you want. I could not care less."

It was night when I left with Trifonof. All along the road to Lyon the population was awake and in the streets. The Germans had retreated a few hours before, but according to the information we gathered some troops remained in the suburbs and were fighting with the Maquis. They were preparing to blow up the bridges. Indeed, soon we heard a series of earthshaking explosions resounding through the night. Bridges worth hundreds of millions of dollars went into the air. I was thinking of Commandant Marey and his attacks of rage at this moment. Perhaps the French commander too was regretting not having followed Marey's advice. My only consolation was to learn over the radio that the American column in the east was proceeding straight northward. I wondered if I would ever know whether this move was connected with the information found in the German officer's billfold.

We drove from village to village, shouting our appeals for surrender over the loudspeaker, but the Germans had gone. In one hamlet, a group of citizens handed us a German soldier who had been hiding in a barn. We took him between us on our truck's front seat.

At dawn, on 2 September 1944, we witnessed a strange scene: thousands of young men, mostly unarmed, were proceeding in two columns along the main road to Lyon. They wore armbands of the F.T.P.F. *(francs tireurs et partisans français),* the leftist partisan forces which had probably been instructed to take the city and inscribe this victory to their credit. But they were soon overtaken by the armored cars of the First French Army, which had left Givors at daybreak. We managed to tuck our truck between two tanks and thus entered the city among the first vehicles. An almost indescribable scene then took place: thousands of citizens flocked to the vehicles, embracing the French soldiers, offering them flowers, all expressing in their individual way their joy at liberation, a real explosion of pent-up frustrations and outworn patience over the long years of occupation. Placed as we were and wearing the underground's uniforms we were engulfed in this outburst of joy. I remember a man handing me a can of gasoline he had

saved for the liberation and a woman presenting me with
her infant to bless! Girls put their heads through the windows of our truck and kissed us frantically, including our
German prisoner, who could not escape from the general
wave of emotion and began to cry like a child. But this scene
did not last long, for suddenly a cataract of shots crackled
from the roofs of the city across the Saône River. Another
apocalyptic scene then unfolded before our eyes:

The same thousands of people were fleeing back to
their houses and back streets, while many of them threw
themselves flat on the road and on the sidewalks. I will
never forget the image of a fleshy woman sobbing spasmod-
ically, her face against the ground, and her skirt high up,
revealing her large white bottom bulging in vast oversized
pink panties. Women were shouting and moaning in an-
guish, looking for their children, while young Maquisards
were firing their Sten guns like madmen from behind the
walls along the river. It was such a great occasion for them
to try their guns, even if the bullets did not reach the other
side of the large river. Slowly the crowd managed to go
home, while German sharpshooters continued to fire from
attics in the high houses of the inner city. They had to be
captured or killed one by one in house searches by soldiers
and underground forces. They were mostly Germans in
uniform, left behind to effectuate this retarding operation.
But the word also spread rapidly that many Germans were
still in the city to commit murder and sabotage, dressed in
civilian clothes.

There was only one small bridge left to cross the river
Saône and to enter the main part of the city: the Pont de
l'Homme de la Roche, which had been saved by French
resistance fighters. We decided to wait there for the arrival
of our comrades, smoking cigarettes and exchanging a few
words from time to time. We had gotten rid of our German
prisoner, whom we had handed over to the local militia.

Suddenly I felt the point of a gun in my back and heard the order: *"Haut les mains"* (hands up). The same was happening to Trifonof. I asked for explanations but received none, and we were taken by underground men to a police station. There I learned that we had been under observation for a while, that I looked like a German and that we were overheard speaking German with each other. I explained to them that I was from Alsace-Lorraine, that Trifonof was a Russian who understood only German and that we were waiting for the arrival of our main underground group. I had no difficulty in convincing them of the truth and we were set free. We regained our truck and felt that the best course was to return to Givors. On the way back we would watch out for our comrades in case they were proceeding to Lyon.

But they were not, for they had been ordered to stay in Givors where Commandant Marey was acting like a caged tiger.

When we returned to Givors, I learned of the gruesome incident of the execution of twenty young Germans whom we had captured a few days before (see "Nightguard at Givors" in *Most of All, They Taught Me Happiness*).

This was the last incident of my life in the French underground. Our group was repatriated to St. Etienne in the Loire. After a few days my Russians came to say goodbye: they had decided to join the leftist Maquis and were impatiently awaiting their repatriation to the Soviet Union. I took leave with tears of these brave men, my experienced elders, who had protected me like a brother and had probably saved my life several times.

We stayed in St. Etienne doing practically nothing, demoralized by inaction and by rumors that there might be a civil war, that the coal miners of the region were stocking arms and that our group might have to fight a possible

Communist insurgence. When our underground group was finally merged with the regular army, I decided to take leave and to return to Alsace-Lorraine where my parents were still living in the midst of the combat zone, which had stabilized there for the winter.

Of all my underground period, there remains only a trifle of souvenirs: the German revolver taken from an officer in Estivareilles, the billfold in which I found the information on the defenses of Lyon and a few sheets of paper on which I had jotted down the type and numbers of our parachuted arms. Writing this story forty years later, I went to search for these memorabilia in order to convince myself that I was not dreaming and that these events had actually happened. I was reassured about my memory when my hands touched the German officer's billfold and its torn lining. . . .

There is a footnote to this story. As I mentioned earlier, in 1947, while I was studying at the University of Strasbourg, I won an essay contest on world government which earned me a summer internship with the World Federation of United Nations Associations in Geneva, Switzerland, and later employment with the United Nations. The program was directed by Jan Mazaryk from Czechoslovakia. Upon its conclusion, I was invited to the general assembly of the World Federation at Marianske Lazne, in Czechoslovakia. There, one day, I was introduced to a tall, handsome American during a reception given by Jan Mazaryk at the Hradschin Palace. We spoke about the war, and the American soon told me of his respect for the French underground. He said:

"One day we received from a French group the details of the defenses of the city of Lyon. As a result we were able to proceed straight to the north instead of converging sideward with the French troops to Lyon. The information we received probably shortened the war by a day or two, since we could soon afterward capture the stronghold of Belfort."

I commented:

"These defenses were as follows: thirty infantrymen with two antiaircraft guns on the road from Givors, a platoon of soldiers with three antiaircraft guns on the road from Vienne, and similar defenses on the road from Chambéry. All bridges to be blown up."

He looked at me in utter surprise:

"How do you know?"

I told him my story and how delighted I was to learn that the information had reached the Americans after all and that it did have the hoped effect.

He commented:

"I was the commander of the American armored car column and I personally received your information!"

He said that he wanted to get an American medal for me, but I answered that I had no merit whatsoever.

My only regret is that I did not keep more memorabilia from this period of my life, especially the thin piece of paper on which the defenses of Lyon were written down. Today it would be a valuable document for the historians of the city of Lyon and of World War II. But as a tribute to my Russian comrades I will reproduce here their names and the identification of their American arms, the record of which I have kept as the chief of their unit:

Gregory Trifonof	:	a machine gun No. FA 42366
Ilia Nikitin	:	" " No. FA 44252
Teregulof	:	" " No. FA 43529
Nuri Akshurin	:	" " No. FA 60987
Kolia Safin	:	a heavy machine gun 12 T 5882; also in charge of Russian cannon 12 T 5608

Hamid Vallulin	:	assistant to artillerist Safin; a Colt revolver
Boris Garipof	:	an American carbine No. 46 15 872
Jasha Abourachmanof	:	" " " No. 46 135 90
Micha Abushaief	:	" " " No. 46 10 873
Marco (myself)	:	" " " No. 26 67 390.

18

Of Bombardments

*Why do humans inflict such inhuman suffer-
ings upon each other? Do we have to be worse
than animals?*

I will group together in one story all my experiences with
bombardments. They will show that once war and hatred
are unleashed, there is no limit to human imagination and
cruelty in devising ways to hurt one another. It makes me
feel better each morning when I go to the UN to think that
there is now at least for the first time on this planet a group
of world servants whose task it is to try to prevent war, to
work for peace and to promote international cooperation. If
people were really wise, they would press their governments relentlessly and forcefully for a strengthening of
humanity's first world organization and international civil
service. It could make the difference between peace and
war.

My first acquaintance with bombardments started with
old-fashioned artillery. In 1939, when we took refuge behind the combat zone in the little village of Trois-Maisons,
one evening I heard a strange, deep, rolling thunder on the
horizon. My mother became still and said to me:

"Listen, son. Those are the cannons shooting on the
front."

And we remained silent, lost in thought. In my mind I
could see dear homes destroyed which it had taken years to

build and to enrich with hard-won savings, labor and love. I could see soldiers hiding in trenches in order to avoid being killed. I tried to visualize where my father was at that moment and what he might be doing to protect himself. I could see soldiers in different uniforms shoving shining artillery shells into huge guns, praying that they would kill as many enemies as possible. Yes, to meditate during a bombardment can be quite an experience! My mother told me how they listened to similar rolling thunder during World War I. For the children the word "front" had mysterious and frightening connotations. Everyone knew exactly where the front was located and in which direction it was moving.

My second experience was closer to home. We had moved from our first place of refuge to the city of Metz, where I pursued my high school studies. One night, we were suddenly awakened by an enormous explosion in the pitch-black, sleeping and silent city. That was all. There was no further explosion. My mother wondered: "What was that? Could it be the explosion of a gas reservoir in the city, or what else?" She looked at her watch. I knew what she thought, for I was well read in the history of the first world war. I asked her:

"Could it be the Big Bertha?"

"I am afraid so. If in exactly another quarter of an hour there is a new explosion, then there will be no doubt about it."

And indeed, there was. Every fifteen minutes for the remainder of the night, an enormous artillery bomb fell on the city, shot from many miles away inside Germany by a gigantic cannon mounted on railroad tracks. After each shot, the monster withdrew into a railroad tunnel, to hide and to get ready for the next round. The size of that cannon inspired the same sentiment of awe as the sight of the first Zeppelin.

Try to imagine what such nights were like: you live in a city like Des Moines or Boston, and every quarter of an hour, night after night, an enormous bomb explodes somewhere in the city! At first you cannot sleep at all. You imagine the big shell sweeping through the atmosphere and approaching the town. You try to visualize its point of impact. Is it going to be your house, your neighborhood or far away in the city? Will you still be alive in a few minutes? You look at your watch and see the seconds move until the dreadful explosion takes place. At the same instant you know that your house has not been hit and that your life has been spared. But somewhere else, someone is dead or is suffering. You return to your slumber until your senses tell you that danger nears again. After a few days you acquire completely new sleeping habits. My mother, for example, set the alarm clock at fifteen-minute intervals to be awakened and prepared. The Germans then started with similar bombings during the day. The population began either to build underground shelters or to move out of the city. We were among the latter. My mother rented a small apartment in the village of Ars-sur-Moselle, not far from Metz. I rode to school every day on a bicycle. After a few weeks the Big Bertha got tired and it stopped as abruptly as it had started. This remnant of an old technology was soon to be replaced by something much more sophisticated and "efficient": aerial bombardments!

I witnessed the first one as I was riding to school in Metz one morning. Suddenly over the military airport of Metz-Frescati, I noticed a swarm of airplanes. French anti-aircraft batteries began shooting at them and soon I saw a first plane fall down, then a second and a third, followed by violent explosions. The people in the street were applauding at that German defeat. But soon thereafter their joy gave way to consternation: the fallen planes were zooming up again into the sky, while others were diving down almost vertically, dropping their bombs on the airport. We had seen in action Hitler's first squadron of "Stukas," a much dreaded new airplane. It came down with the sound of a siren, was able to break its fall and shoot up again abruptly into the air. This hellish spectacle lasted for about a half-hour. Not a single French airplane was left intact on the base. Similar surprise attacks were taking place on all major French airports. Within an hour France had lost its entire air force. It was the beginning of the excruciating defeat of France by Germany in forty days.

Soon the French troops began to retreat. On my daily bicycle ride to and from Metz, I could see the pillaging of military depots and government factories. Barrels of tobacco and cigarettes were broken up and thrown into the streets. Miles of cigarette paper flew in the wind. Soldiers were shooting in the air, but hordes of people, unperturbed, were shoveling beans, peas and lentils from vast heaps of army stores into empty sacks. I went into the barracks to watch these extraordinary sights. I had never seen the mountains of goods stored by the military, while the civilians had so little. Thus I learned a basic law of human sociology: the military always get everything. What lessons I drew from those sights as a sixteen-year-old boy! It was hard to believe that humans could turn so easily into plunderers and beasts. When I told my mother what I had seen, she was furious that I had not taken a few packs of tobacco for my father, who would be happy to find them during his next furlough. She sent me back to fill a rucksack with them.

One morning in June, I took my last bicycle ride to the school. We were supposed to take the examinations of the baccalaureate, the final exam of high school, the objective of all my efforts and of my mother's sacrifices. But the doors of the school were closed. We waited outside. The principal appeared after a while on the balcony and addressed us pathetically:

"Dear boys, I beg you to go home. Your presence here is futile and dangerous. The German troops are entering Metz at this very moment. I know how hard you have worked and how disappointed you must feel. Life is a tragedy. I love you all. *Vive la France*, our beloved country." And he broke down in tears. I stood there, dumbfounded, incredulous, shuddering under the stark implications of that moment. I could not believe it, although I had seen it coming. I had never thought that I would live such an episode in my life. Twelve years of French high school studies were ending in a void. Hitler, the madman, once again was breaking the peaceful course of my life. A spokesman for the students tried to convince the principal to let us nevertheless take the exams. But it was without avail, and one after the other, we sadly mounted our bicycles and went home.

When I crossed the city, I saw the first German troops arrive: swarms of motorcycles with sidecars, mounted by soldiers whose uniforms were worthy of a James Bond film. I do not know how many persons on this planet have witnessed the arrival of victorious foreign troops. I do not wish anyone to experience it. I remember a curious scene: the German soldiers rushed to a monument commemorating World War I. It showed a French cock in bronze holding a German eagle in its claws. The Germans tore off the group and turned it upside down: now the German eagle was strangling the French cock!

I never returned to French high school. I never finished my regular French secondary studies, missing in particular the last and most interesting course in philosophy, leading to the second baccalaureate. As a result, I had to develop my own philosophy of life, without the help of the great minds who have enlightened the course of human history.

The first phase of the war was over. We returned to our

home in Sarreguemines and started to live under German occupation. A series of new experiences in bombardments began, but this time the bombs came from the other side, especially after the British had built an air force and the U.S. had entered the war.

The people of my hometown were taught how to protect themselves. We built solid underground cellars where we could take refuge, live and sleep during air raids. We were instructed to place pails of sand in the attics in order to fight incendiary bombs. All windows were hermetically sealed, so that no light was visible from the air. Patrols enforced a total blackout at night. At first, the Allied planes flew over the town and carefully avoided bombing Alsace-Lorraine. The British operated at night and the Americans during the day. From our cellar we could hear the deep, long, reverberating sound of the slow-moving, heavy American planes high up in the sky. When they were over the city, German antiaircraft batteries began their pandemonium. After a while the hellish noises subsided. A few hours later one could hear the lighter sound of the planes returning from their targets. Our streets were covered with strips of aluminum foil resembling Christmas icicles. They were thrown from the planes in order to blur the radar of the German antiaircraft batteries.

The population was confident that the Allies would never bomb our town. Often, from the street or from our windows we watched the air battles raging in the sky. One night, I was observing the sky from the entrance of our house when suddenly an enormous dark mass jutted out of nowhere and overflew the house with a shattering sound. Three or four other machines followed. They were British night bombers, specializing in low-altitude bombings. I flattened down on the ground and then saw dozens of sparkling lights burn in the street. They were incendiary bombs. Instinctively I rushed upstairs to the attic to see if any of them had fallen on the house. I found three of them which had crashed through the roof and were burning on the floor, exuding a strong odor of phosphor. With shovelfuls of sand I managed to extinguish them. I then ran downstairs, for I had heard frightened cries in the street. Several houses were on fire. The town was in panic. There was not enough fire equipment to cope with the situation. I had an idea and ran to the prison, which was located near our house, and asked for their fire hose. First they refused because it was government property, but a group of people joined me and soon we ran out of the prison with a long hose on our shoulders. I had a quick look at the burning houses. One of them, where we had lived a few years before, was beyond salvation. The entire roof was on fire. Next to it, another house was just beginning to show short flames licking through the roof. We attached our hose to a fire hydrant and managed to extinguish the fire. Firemen came later to finish the job while we were working on another house. When I returned home and passed in front of our former home, I saw that it had burned to the ground.

I felt happy as a king when I arrived home. I was under the impression that I had done something useful. But my father commented dryly: "You extinguished the wrong house. You should have saved our former home where I kept hidden a few hundred first-grade prewar hat cones. We used them sparingly in exchange for food and other goods on the black market."

Well, it could not be helped and it could have been much worse for our family. My mother then made me aware that I was still in pajamas and that they were burned in several places!

Daytime bombardments were the specialty of the Americans. When the sky was clear, we could see them distinctly, high up in a formation called a "flying fortress": the bombers were in the middle, surrounded and protected by heavily armed combat planes making the whole thing look like a flying porcupine. Light and highly mobile German Messerschmitts shot up in the air and buzzed around them, and sometimes through them, like bees. Their range of action was very short and soon they abandoned the scene, replaced by fresh ones. Once in a while a plane was hit and one could see parachutes opening. This always created a turmoil among the Germans. *Feldgendarmes*, motorcyclists and policemen with German shepherds rushed by the dozens to the fields and woods, scanning the region to catch the airmen before they could hide and later cross the border, eventually to return to England.

One day, shortly after American planes had overflown the city, they came back and to the terror of the population they dropped all their bombs on the city. What hell it was! One bomb fell on the house across from ours and killed all its inhabitants. In one of the apartments there lived a young German woman with her child, whom her husband had thought to be safer here than in Germany. He had rented an apartment for them in our town, while he himself was fighting in Russia. I still remember the romantic look of the young blond woman. She was very sad, all alone, without friends. One could often see her leaning out of a window on the ground floor, holding and playing with her child. She looked pale and desperate as if she knew what fate was in store for her.

When the town emerged from its rubble, it counted 170 dead and 630 wounded. I remember our fish merchant running like mad all over the town looking for his wife and three children. They had all been killed under a bridge where they had taken refuge and which had collapsed, hit by a bomb.

From then on, no one felt safe anymore and when air raid sirens started to howl, most people seized their bicycles and fled to the fields until the alarm was over.

Later I got an explanation of what had happened. I had joined the United Nations in New York, when one day I was invited to a cocktail party for the launching of the first book by Norman Mailer. He was a close friend of my chief of section at the United Nations, Karl Lachmann. There were many guests at the party. War was still a fresh subject of conversation. I met a tall American who asked me where I came from in France. When I named my hometown, Sarreguemines, he exclaimed:

"My God! Do I remember Sarreguemines! I wondered if I would ever meet someone from that town. We bombarded it stupidly on one of our missions. I was a pilot in that group. We were to make a raid on Saarbrücken in Germany, which we had bombarded many times before. But this time the German flak was so strong that we could not get through. So we flew back and poured our bombs on the next best town, namely yours.[1] We made an effort, but not a very successful one, to bomb the railroad station and network. Do you know how many people were killed?"

I told him.

What we suffered was of course very little compared with what the Germans went through in their towns. At the end of the war Saarbrücken was but a vast heap of ruins. I remember walking one morning through the city of Ludwigshafen on my way to Heidelberg, the railroad line having been cut by a bombardment. I walked for miles through blocks of houses which had been literally pulverized during the night. I wondered how such total destruction could be achieved. Each block was simply flattened out, one square of desolate and smoldering ruins following the other. Someone gave me the explanation: the British first sprinkled the

---

[1.] It was a similar dropping of bombs on a Belgian town which prompted a U.S. bomber pilot, Gary Davis, to declare himself the first world citizen and to devote his life to fighting the nation-state system.

town with incendiary bombs and a few hours later when the city was in flames, causing a strong upward draft of hot air, they returned and dropped explosive bombs right into the middle of the furnace. The strength of the explosion, multiplied by the upward draft, was such that it blew down anything that was still standing! Never in my life will I forget my walk early after sunrise through these cataclysmic fields of ruins and groups of crying people. Germans or not, these were all human brothers and sisters suffering inhuman pains inflicted upon them by other humans. What an insane world it was! Humanity was much worse than the animal kingdom. And God's beautiful resurrected sun was shining impassively on those horrible scenes. Was there really a God in heaven?

I was still to witness another change in the direction of the bombs before the war was over. On the eve of New Year 1945, I spent a few days in my grandfather's village, Sarralbe, trying to pass through American military controls in order to join my parents in Sarreguemines where the front had stabilized at the onset of winter. I was staying with my uncle René Muller and we spent every night in a concrete bunker built by the Germans near the Solvay salt and nitrate works. The Germans were again using a Big Bertha located somewhere in Germany in a railroad tunnel! Every quarter of an hour, as in Metz almost five years before, I heard the impact of a bomb catapulted against the small locality occupied by the American troops. The bombs penetrated deep into the earth and lifted with their explosion several houses at the same time! During the day we also often heard strange noises in the sky, resembling those of a flying harvester: they were the German V-2s on their way to England!

These were my last experiences with bombardments. For a long time to come, people in Alsace-Lorraine would remember such events and talk about them, mourning

their dead and healing their wounds. Progressively, peace returned, the rubble was cleared, cities were reconstructed, the dead were forgotten and youngsters were born who barely listened to the stories told by their elders. And in the vast power game of nations, new candidates appeared, replacing the former ones, and the bitter political competition for illusory power under which we had suffered so much in Europe started all over again, embracing this time the entire planet. Conflicts erupted in different parts of the globe, in Africa and in Asia. In Viet Nam more bombs were dropped than all the bombs of World War I and II. The high skies of our planet are now infested with planes carrying atomic bombs on a round-the-clock basis. Our seas and oceans are marauded by submarines carrying missiles capable of killing the entire human race ten times and more. It is true, the Big Berthas have disappeared, but hundreds of deadly intercontinental missiles are lurking in the ground, tested every twenty seconds by computer as to their readiness and "good" functioning. And yet, four and a half billion people arise passively every morning and go to bed peacefully every evening without screaming their fear and disgust at the governments who foster such insanity, squandering hundreds of billions of dollars in the midst of horrid poverty, and still wanting to be admired as great powers and leaders of peoples! If an inspection team from outer space were to visit us, I am sure they would conclude that this was definitely not the way to run a planet.

At least there is one consolation: in another war no one will have to go through the ordeal of one of our distant relatives. She had taken refuge with her parents and grandparents in a village in the combat zone near Bitche. A bomb fell into the cellar and lodged itself in the belly of the grandfather, whom it killed instantly, but it did not explode. The family had to wait for several days until soldiers came to defuse and remove the bomb and the body. The military of

today can at least reassure us that such malfunctionings will never occur again and that we can count with certitude on instant death. Thank you, thank you very much, gentlemen of the military "art," for your good progress and your concern for human suffering!

19

General Patton Did Not Sleep Here

*The greatest joy on earth is an entire family
alive and unharmed after a war.*

It was 31 December 1944. I had not been able to reach my
hometown in time for Christmas. Sarreguemines was still in
the combat zone and I had been trying in vain for two or
three days, ten miles away from it, in Sarralbe, to get
through U.S. military controls. At long last I was lucky. I
tried hitchhiking, and an American officer stopped and
asked me if I knew the region. "Like my pocket," I answered, "I have lived here most of my life." He invited me
to hop into his car. I was loaded with loaves of bread and
sausages, since I knew that there was a severe shortage of
food in the combat zone. We drove to Sarreguemines, using
all the side roads I knew in order to avoid roadblocks and
the American military police, which so far had been turning
me back. The trip ended without incident and the U.S.
officer deposited me right in front of our house on the outskirts of the city. My first anxious look was to see if our good
home was still standing, and thanks to the Lord, after five
years of war, there it was, offering all its beauty and moving
memories to my avid eyes.

I found my parents and sister hiding in the cellar, but
they were together and alive. They had decided to stay at

home instead of fleeing with the majority of the population to vast underground caves in the riverbank of the Sarre, whence the people now could not escape because the Germans across the river covered the exit routes with their guns. How several thousand people lived for more than a month in these caves had been much written about in the media. Children were born, people died and were buried, surgery was performed, collective kitchens fed the refugees, and some of the rich merchants even built small wooden houses or barracks in the caves. Love and hatred, life and death, greed and altruism, all the good and evil of a human society had accompanied the people into their underground refuge. The only bonds that held them together were their instinct for survival and the fear of the combat raging in the city.

Words are inadequate to describe the joy of our family's reunion and what it meant to each of us, perhaps in a different way: for my mother it was the reunion and survival of her family; for my father the triumph of his tireless efforts; for my sister the end of a nightmare; and for me the petering out of a great historical nonsense and colossal waste of time. But the miracle was accomplished: we had survived, we were alive, unharmed and reunited. The long, tortuous path filled with dangers, fears, ruses, suffering and accommodations that led us there was irrelevant. We all knew that only the result counted and we enjoyed tremendously this family victory: the survival of the tribe amid a cataclysmic fight of giants. We were all alive and unharmed!

We spent the rest of the day and a good part of the night telling each other what had happened during our fifteen long months of separation. It is true, we had been able to write to each other once in a while through friends and relatives on both sides of the border. In our correspondence I used a girl's name, Georgette, from my middle name of George. But we had carefully kept all the bad news from each other in order not to make life even more miserable. Thus I now learned that my father had been in prison for more than a year because I had fled. My mother had decided to hide this fact from me, knowing that I would have immediately surrendered to the Germans, a gesture which would not have helped much. My father had been freed only a few days before when the Germans panicked, retreated from our side of the city and fled to the other bank of the river. The main American armored forces were stalled sixty kilometers behind, in Nancy, by a lack of gasoline.

I told my parents my adventures in the underground. They had of course guessed that I was not living comfortably with one of my uncles as I had written in my letters. But there again it would not have helped to tell them the truth and have worried them unduly.

We celebrated our reunion and the New Year happily in our cellar, while fighting was raging in the city. The cellar was safe and reasonably comfortable: a wooden platform tightly held up the ceiling as a protection against the effects of a bombardment. There were bunk beds, acetylene lamps, a reserve of food, sandboxes against incendiary bombs, and picks and shovels to dig out from the rubble if necessary.

My father extracted from his hidden reserve a good bottle of prewar French wine and my mother cooked a fine meal in the laundry room, which had been transformed into a kitchen since it was too dangerous to live on the upper floor. As I was watching her cook, my eyes were scanning around, trying to remember familiar scenes and objects from my youth. Suddenly I caught sight of a bazooka leaning in a corner of the laundry room. I asked my mother:

"What on earth is this weapon doing here?"

"Oh! It is nothing. A German soldier left it behind."

"What do you mean? No German soldier in his right mind would leave a bazooka behind in a civilian home. He would have to account for it dearly."

I sensed that there was a story behind that weapon. I insisted and this is what my mother finally told me:

"Well, you see, when the Germans retreated to the other side of the town they left behind a few soldiers, stationed near street corners and road intersections, to use their bazookas against the advancing American tanks when they came. The latter were bound to use the main road in front of our house. A German soldier was therefore positioned behind our garden wall and he waited for the Americans with his weapon. I was furious, because, despite the damage caused last year by a bomb that fell on the street, our house had on the whole withstood successfully the war. I saw no reason why it should be damaged at the last moment by American tanks. It was bitter cold outside. I asked the young soldier to come in and gave him a cup of coffee and a schnapps to warm up. We talked. I made him speak about his mother. I told him about you and how terrible it was to be a mother in wartimes. After a few cups of coffee and schnapps he became sentimental and homesick. I then asked him:

"What is the point of risking your life at this late hour of the war? Your officers have fled on the other side of the river. Do they expect you to stop the American army with your weapon? Even if you shoot down a tank or two, they will get you and I can already see your dead body lying in my garden. What will I do? Pay a visit to your mother, cry with her and tell her how heroic you were? She would ask me: 'Why didn't you stop him and send him home to me?' If she were here at this moment, she would beg you to drop your bazooka, to cross the river and to go home to her. Soon you will be able to forget this nightmare and to start a new life. The survivors will be happy that they did not die for this nonsense."

Knowing how good a lawyer my mother was for the causes of the family, I could easily guess the outcome:

"Well, he admitted that I was right, thanked me, kissed me on behalf of his mother, asked me for another schnapps, handed me his bazooka and left for Germany."

I congratulated her on this achievement and asked her another question which was burning my lips:

"How is it that for the first time in this war our house is not occupied by soldiers? We had a French general, we had German troops and I expected to see the place swarming with Americans. What happened?"

"Good question," she answered. "They came all right and tried to requisition the house a few days ago. A group of officers knocked at the door and asked me if their general could use the house as his headquarters. I said that I lived here alone with your sister and that it would not be proper for officers and soldiers to stay with women under the same roof. To my great surprise they accepted my point of view, saluted me and left! This is the first time in this bloody war that I met with real gentlemen!"

I asked her:

"What was the name of their general?"

"General Patton."

I jumped!

"What! You turned down General Patton? For the first time a famous general would have lived in this house and you refused him accommodation? After the war you could have had a plaque affixed on the house, saying: 'General Patton slept here.' "

But she could not have cared less, tired as she was of all wars, soldiers, generals and uniforms. She jokingly commented: "Well, you can have a plaque affixed saying: 'General Patton did *not* sleep here,' " which I am doing in a way today writing this story.

Speaking of generals, I had noticed that a picture of General de Gaulle was hanging in the entrance hall, hiding a niche in the wall where the electrical switches and fuses of the house were located. When I had left for France, there was a picture of Hitler at that spot. Under Nazi occupation it was mandatory to have a picture of him in all houses, and my father thought that there he would at least serve a useful purpose, hiding the unbecoming sight of the instruments. Seized by a sudden suspicion, I turned de Gaulle's picture around and, sure enough, found Hitler on the other side!

My mother blushed a little and commented:

"Well, the Germans are still across the river and they might come back from one moment to another!"

Once again I recognized my mother's overriding sense for family survival!

We spent a good part of the night celebrating, and then went to sleep, knocked out by our emotions, the good French wine and the heavy Alsatian cooking. At one point, loud and intensive shooting in the street woke me up. I noticed that my mother was wide awake. She said to me as if I were still a little boy:

"Do not worry, son. It has been like this every night during the last few days. You are just not accustomed to the shooting!"

What were her real thoughts and feelings at that moment? She probably could not sleep, as the film of so many years of war and suffering unfolded in her mind. Now, at long last, the whole family was united and safe, and the end of the war was near. But her clear, blue eyes were still scanning a bomb shelter and her ears were listening to the sounds of deadly weapons. . . .

In the morning we learned that the Germans had recaptured the town but were driven back by the Americans at dawn.[1] After all my tribulations and efforts to escape from the Germans I had spent my first night at home and New Year's Eve right in the middle of them!

[1] In 1981, I was able to trace most of the American officers who ran our town from December 1944 to March 1945. We had a reunion in my home and they were invited by my town on 6 December 1981, anniversary of its liberation by American troops. A Major Bennett Square was inaugurated to honor their commander, later killed in action.

20

A Family Balance Sheet

We must take stock and transform our adversities into positive contributions.

How did our larger family fare during those five years of war? Did we suffer any losses? What was our tribal position in the total balance sheet of the world holocaust?

My father and mother each had four brothers or sisters. Of the nine families they founded, three remained in France and did not return to Alsace-Lorraine when Hitler occupied the provinces. Five others returned to their evacuated homes on the border. Only one family, which lived in Metz, a city sufficiently far behind the front, had not been forced to leave its home. Of the nine male heads of these families, five served in the French army during 1939–40, but they were beyond German enlistment age. Of the fourteen children of the nine families, eight were girls, and six were boys. Four of the boys reached military age during the war, namely myself in Lorraine and three cousins in Alsace. I will briefly tell their stories.

My cousin from Strasbourg, Eugene Schneider, was studying engineering at the University of Karlsruhe. He was able to obtain several postponements for study purposes, since Germany badly needed a new generation of engineers. But toward the end of the war no one was exempted any longer and he finally had to join the German army. His father did not allow him to flee to France. He served for about a year on the Russian front, was wounded during the battle of Stalingrad and repatriated in one of the last German planes that left the battleground during the Nazi retreat.

My two other cousins, Simon and Eugene Hermann, were the sons of farmers who lived in Kilstett, a little village near the Rhine River to the north of Strasbourg. One was a railroad worker, the other an apprentice electrician. The first managed to cross the border on a train engine, as I had done. He reached North Africa where he joined the First French Army, the same army that landed in the south of France, went up the Rhone Valley and liberated Alsace under the command of General de Lattre de Tassigny. With a little luck we could have met in Givors or in Lyon! His parents were not deported, for they were peasants and Hitler needed the peasants to stay and till the land.

The younger brother did not escape and was enlisted in the German army. By some extraordinary circumstance he was sent with an infantry regiment to France! The thought of escaping did not occur to him, for he was not fluent in French and would not have known where to go. One day, in Normandy, he was carrying food from a village to a German outpost when he met soldiers on the side of a road. He greeted them in German. The soldiers flattened behind a hedge and mowed him down with a machine gun and hand grenades. They were Americans. He was later picked up by an American ambulance. He had escaped death by a miracle, but his hips and legs were badly smashed. He was shipped to England where surgery was performed on him. The International Red Cross repatriated him in exchange for severely wounded English prisoners. Some of the best German surgeons worked on him in Heidelberg. When the war was over, he came home as a cripple, but after several further operations in Strasbourg he was able to walk again, having regained the partial use of his legs.

When I saw him last in 1980, I asked him how many times he had been operated on: "Eight times, and a doctor has seen me twice a week for the last thirty-five years!" Since it was summer he was not wearing long sleeves and I saw that his arms were dotted with innumerable bloody red spots. I asked him what they were. He answered: "They are metal splinters which are still coming out of my body. I have them all over." Thirty-five years later! Can you imagine the misery of that man during so many years! Can we imagine the number of veterans on this planet who are going through similar agonies as a result of wars? While the same humanity has still not been able to eradicate malnutrition, which is responsible for 100 million of the 450 million handicapped on this planet, we offer ourselves the luxury of causing needless, inhuman disabilities by engaging in stupid, totally incomprehensible and unforgivable wars. Cousin Eugene was by far the unluckiest of the family and he will be relieved of his miseries only by death.

When the two brothers came home in 1945 they found their village surrounded by a sea of destroyed and damaged American and German tanks: Kilstett had been the site of one of the fiercest tank battles of World War II. German SS troops had been ordered by Hitler to cross the Rhine and to recapture Strasbourg, and French troops equipped with American tanks had been ordered by de Gaulle to stop them at all cost. The wife of my uncle Emile in Strasbourg had sent her little son to Kilstett, which she thought was safer than the big city. The boy lost an eye and a piece of his skull during the battle and to this day his brain is protected by a silver disk.

A few weeks after the war everyone in the family had returned home, except my youngest uncle, Emile. He was a tall, stocky railroad workman in his thirties, too old to be a regular soldier, but still young enough to be used by the Germans. They enlisted him in the police force and sent him to the Oder-Neisse region of Poland, where they employed police regiments instead of regular troops to keep the population under control.

We waited for him anxiously for several months. His wife had no news from him whatsoever. We tried every possible channel, including the International Red Cross in Geneva. After a year, we gave up hope. His wife began to wear black mourning clothes and we sadly concluded that one of us had not made it. His little son would probably never see his father again.

Then suddenly, one day, after we had abandoned all hope, we learned that he had shown up at his home, to the great joy of his wife and son. We all rushed to Strasbourg to find out what had happened. This is what he told us:

He was stranded in the German-speaking part of Poland when the Russians began their advance toward Germany. One day, he found himself hiding in a wood with a comrade from Saarbrücken when Russian tanks crossed the wood. His friend wanted to surrender, but he thought that it was too risky. His comrade went ahead, held his arms up, walked toward the tanks and was mowed down instantly. My uncle reflected about his situation: here he was, far from home, in a region entirely occupied by the Russians, unable to communicate with them and explain that he was a Frenchman from Alsace-Lorraine. He was running the same risk of being shot if he surrendered. When he was mobilized, the Germans had tattooed an identification number on his forearm. The Russians would take him for a member of the SS and have him executed forthwith. He decided to ask for help at an isolated German farmhouse. The family that lived there agreed to harbor him. Their own son had not returned from the war and they hoped that someone somewhere would assist him similarly, if he was still alive. They gave him civilian clothes and he helped them as a farmhand. He stayed always inside the farm and whenever a visitor came he took refuge in a haystack. He stayed with that family for over a year until things had settled down. Then the peasant one day said to him:

"Let us go to Warsaw and try to contact the French authorities. You will explain to them your situation and they will repatriate you."

The peasant loaded a wagon with sacks of potatoes for sale in the city. My uncle hid under them and off they went to Warsaw. The peasant drove around in the city until he saw a French officer of the Allied Command. He told him what had brought him to Warsaw. The French officer led them to the French Embassy where my uncle explained his situation. A few days later he was repatriated to Strasbourg. When he knocked at the door of his home, his wife almost fainted from the shock.

This was the end of the ordeal. Everybody in the family was home and alive. Only three relatives had been wounded, one of them crippled for life. Only one home, namely that of my grandfather, had suffered severe destruction. Two others were partly damaged. All the personal belongings of eight of the nine families had been destroyed or lost. Each of us later in life remembered many a cherished object, be it a family souvenir, a stamp collection, a portrait, a book or a toy, but all these losses were nothing compared with the fact that we had survived the deadly holocaust. We could all now take renewed hope in the future, resume our activities, rebuild what had been destroyed, return to school, plan our lives, found new families, enter a profession and continue the endless chain of human joys and sufferings on planet earth. God, in His kindness, had reserved for me a wonderful life right in the center of world affairs. I would be privileged to know most of the world, deal with almost every conceivable human problem, devote my entire adulthood not to any single nation but to the whole human family, give vent to my dreams, thoughts, love and action for all that was good and beautiful on our planet. My fate was to be linked with one of the greatest attempts ever to build permanent peace and a decent world during one of the most complex, dangerous but also most exciting and promising periods of human evolution. There would still be many local conflicts and unnecessary human sufferings, but there would be no more world wars. Every child in Europe could go to sleep every evening without having to fear a war the following morning. Peoples from North and South, East and West, blacks and whites, rich and poor, believers and nonbelievers began to gather and to work together in the first worldwide organization. We were entering the first global age of our planet. Individual and family balance sheets could henceforth unfold within better national and world balance sheets. For the first time ever there was a good chance for the advent of a peaceful, orderly and happy human society. After all the trouble I had gone through, I was privileged to live right at the center of this extraordinary new page of human history and to try to help prevent the recurrence of all the horrors I had known.

Yes, when the ordeal was over, I reflected profoundly about its significance and about my future. Would I become a medical doctor as I had intended to before the war, or a hat maker who would take over the family business as my father wanted me to? No, I had to do something about this insane world. I would work for peace. When I said that to my father he laughed: "How on earth can you, the son of a modest hat maker, dream of working for peace? You must have gone mad!" But I knew from experience and from the teachings of Dr. Coué that dreams always come true if one believes in them long enough and works hard. So I went to the University of Strasbourg to study law and economics, and in 1947, riding in a train from Strasbourg to my hometown, I remembered an announcement I had seen at the university for an essay contest on world government. I wrote my essay and in 1948 entered the United Nations, where I have worked ever since.

21

The Young Soldier

Let no war deprive a wife of her husband.

If God permits, I will continue with further stories and highlights of my life experiences at the United Nations in other volumes.

My service with the UN peacekeeping forces in Cyprus would alone fill an entire volume, and so would my years of collaboration with three Secretaries-General. I will add here only a few anecdotes relating to World Wars I and II.

One such anecdote concerns the visit to the United Nations in the 1970s of Mr. Beauguitte, the mayor of Verdun, a French city made famous by World War I. He had come to New York as a member of France's delegation to the UN General Assembly. I thought that it would be interesting to arrange a radio interview for him, since he was still living amid the preserved ruins of one of the most gruesome battlefields the world has ever known. What would he have to say about war and peace, the reconciliation of France and Germany, the Europe of today and the state of the world?

He accepted gladly. While we were waiting for the broadcast to begin, we had occasion for a chat during which I learned that he had known Aristide Briand, the famous French statesman, orator and internationalist of the 1920s.

"He was a friend of my father and he often came to our house during weekends," said Mr. Beauguitte. "He used to test his famous speeches to the League of Nations on private persons or audiences. I served at that time as a special assistant to my father, who was prefect of the region north of Paris. Briand liked to try his speeches on me and to hear through my mouth the comments of the younger generation. A few days later I could read the speeches in the newspapers and I was very proud to detect sometimes the influence of my comments. Briand's fame, idealism, and magnetic personality prompted me to enter politics myself, and I have uninterruptedly served the city of Verdun as mayor, and the French Parliament as congressman, for more than forty years."

I told him how deeply Verdun had impressed me when I visited it for the first time with my father, as a boy. I had heard many stories about the savage battles between Germans and French which had raged for almost four years around that town. One of my uncles, Alphonse Schaeffer, told me of the ordeals he had gone through as a German soldier in the trenches. He had survived only because one day he found himself alone with another man from Alsace-Lorraine in a bomb crater without any Germans around. They decided to shoot at each other, one in the leg, the other through the hand in order to be evacuated as wounded. The scars were still visible on my uncle's palm and they left a tremendous impression on me. Another relative, Jean Bogenschütz, decided in Verdun never to set foot again in a church as long as he lived. He had found it unacceptable to be asked to kill French brothers in the name of God. German soldiers at that time wore buckles with the inscription: *"Gott mit uns"* (God is with us).[1] When

---

[1] The Russian soldiers, too, had buckles with the inscription *"Bog s nami"* (God is with us). The English and the Belgians had the motto *"Dieu et mon Droit"* (God and my right); the Americans, "God and my country." Every nation wants to have God and right on its side, while the world and

after days and nights in cold, wet trenches, the exhausted soldiers were allowed to walk back for miles for a rest in the rear, the first thing they had to do was to attend mass and listen to the patriotic sermon of a German priest! My cousin swore at that time never to listen again to a priest and not to set foot in any house of worship as long as he lived. I could perfectly understand his feelings and I believe that people all around the world should follow his example and leave a religion which takes the side of war and killing.

When I visited the battlefield in 1935, one could still find weapons on the grounds, and I kept from my visit a rusty but well-preserved rifle. I had the joy of finding it in an attic when I visited our old home in Sarreguemines in the summer of 1982.

Two things struck me most in Verdun. One was the famous Trench of Bayonets, in which a platoon of French soldiers had been buried alive by artillery. The tips of their bayonets emerging from the ground are still visible today, the whole trench having been made a shrine protected by a roof of concrete. The second was the bone house or ossuary of Douaumont, a memorial building several hundred feet long, surmounted by a lighthouse beaming in all directions at night, and containing unbelievable mountains of human bones gathered from the various battlefields. One can see their dreadful heaps through windows in the cellars. I remember saying to my father that if another war should ever be about to break out, the world's political leaders should be locked up in one of these cellars until they made peace. This was in 1935. Five years later hell broke out again all over Europe.

---

humanity are left high and dry. I have never heard anyone say: God and the United Nations. And yet, shouldn't the UN become the "holy family of nations" as Secretary-General Pérez de Cuéllar once declared?

The mention of the name Douaumont prompted Mr. Beauguitte to tell me the following story:

"Recently our Public Works Department was excavating the ground near the ossuary in order to lay some underground pipes. One morning I was called to the site because the workers had discovered the body of a soldier from World War I. He was kneeling in a hole, holding a rifle in his arms and wearing a blue coat and red pants, which were the uniform of the French infantry at the beginning of the war. He had probably been buried alive by a bomb and preserved by underground water and soil with a favorable chemical composition. Soon after the discovery, the cloth disintegrated and all that was left were his bones, an identification bracelet and a chain locket containing the enameled picture of a young woman. We checked the war records of the Ministry of Defense in Paris. The number engraved on the bracelet allowed us to find his name, age and place of origin, a small town in northern France. He was a very young soldier, only eighteen years old. I sent my deputy to this town to ascertain if there was still any family left. He discovered that the young soldier had been married and that his widow was still alive! He found her address and decided to visit her. He met an elderly lady with gray hair, living all alone in a one-room apartment. He told her gently about the discovery and handed her the locket. She opened it and after a long silence she commented:

" 'Do you see this lovely young girl? Well, it was me. We were only married for a few short weeks when he left for the war, and I never saw him again. All I possess from him is this picture.' And she pointed at a large framed photograph of a handsome young man, occupying the center of a wall.

"She added sadly: 'I have remained alone ever since then. I never remarried.' "

The time had come for Mayor Beauguitte to speak over the UN radio. He set aside the notes he had prepared and made a moving plea for disarmament and the banning of all weapons and wars. Aristide Briand, the ruins of Verdun, the mounds of human bones, the ghost of the young French soldier and the sorrows of his widow were all speaking through his lips, and the listeners probably wondered why this man's voice was so filled with emotion. While he spoke, I thought of the millions of dead, of widows, orphans and cripples caused by wars all over this planet since the young soldier was buried alive in Douaumont. A war was still raging in Viet Nam and fighting had broken out again in the Middle East. Senseless, brutal killing, wounding and destruction were still being waged by several nations in the name of right, justice, peace and future happiness. Political sanity had not made much progress on power-drunk planet earth. There was still need to lock up the leaders in one of the cellars of the bone house in Douaumont.

But my indomitable optimism and faith in humanity soon took over again and when Mr. Beauguitte finished his broadcast I said to him:

"Mr. Mayor, you must have met uncounted soldiers and veterans of war during your life. But have you ever met any peace soldiers? Allow me to take you tonight to a reception at which you will meet a general and several officers of the UN peace-keeping forces. They still represent only a small fraction of our planet's total military establishment, but there have already been some 50,000 "soldiers without enemies" who have served the blue flag and worn the blue helmets and berets of the United Nations in various parts of the world. I believe the mayor of Verdun should meet some of them."

He accompanied me in the evening to a reception offered by General Rikhye, the Indian president of the International Peace Academy, a former commander of the UN forces in the Middle East and adviser to Secretary-General Hammarskjöld. The general told the mayor that a European branch of the academy had just been opened in Menton, France, in order to train young diplomats and officers from Europe and Africa in the arts of peacemaking and peace-keeping. When he heard that, Mr. Beauguitte said:

"General, on your next visit to France, please come to Verdun. President de Gaulle has instituted a peace medal which I am empowered to confer upon anyone I deem worthy of it. Nothing would please me more than to bestow it upon the first peace general ever to visit Verdun."

Another tiny circle had closed itself in my life. In a corner of my mind I made a mental note: "At one point, suggest to General Rikhye to hold a meeting of the International Peace Academy in Verdun, preferably in the bone house of Douaumont."

22

Sons of Bitche

I hope to be declared someday a true Son of Bitche for peace.

One day in the 1950s, shortly after our marriage, my wife and I had dinner in Greenwich Village, New York's Montmartre. At a table next to ours sat an American couple. The young man had already had numerous drinks. He tried to engage in a conversation with us. But we pretended not to know English and spoke French in order not to get involved with him. At one point, wanting to break the ice between us, he pulled an identity card from his wallet and placed it right under my eyes. He uttered a few words in French trying to explain that he had been a soldier in France. I examined the card and read it with astonishment: the mayor of the city of Bitche, a locality not far from my hometown of Sarreguemines, had certified that private so and so was a . . . son of Bitche! The card had a photograph and all the marks of a serious, official document. The young man explained to me that he had been a soldier under Patton in 1944 and that truckloads of Americans fighting in that region had gone to Bitche to receive such certificates. I gave him his card back and he chuckled with delight when he saw the surprise written all over my face.

When I mentioned this episode to a friend of mine, Leon Buchheit, an Alsace-Lorrainer who had emigrated from Bitche to the United States, he told me that there existed an association of "Sons of Bitche" in America, which held a convention each year!

During our following home leave in France I drove to the town of Bitche to pay a visit to the mayor. Bitche is a famous fortified city in northeastern France with a long military history. Hundreds of thousands of French and African soldiers have been trained on its grounds. During the second world war it was one of the main targets of the American winter offensive of 1944. I knew the mayor from an electoral campaign we had conducted for General de Gaulle in the region in 1951. When I told him about our encounter with the young American in Greenwich Village, he remembered indeed that numerous American soldiers had flocked to his town after the battle to receive such certificates. An office had even been established in city hall to issue them. He had signed them all, but never really understood why the soldiers wanted them so eagerly.

I explained to him the double meaning of the words "son of bitch[e]," which made the possession of such certificates an invaluable gag, and I told him that there even existed an association of Sons of Bitche in the United States. Whereupon he said:

"This explains why an American group approached me shortly after the war with an offer to pay for a free trip to the United States for one of our citizens. Unfortunately, they offered a plane trip and of course no one in our town was willing to take a plane at that time. If they had offered us a boat trip I would have had no difficulty in finding someone."

Later, whenever I heard the expression s.o.b. in the United States, I invariably thought of those American soldiers who in the middle of battle had the sense of humor to devise such a witty gag. How many are still alive today? Does the Association of S.O.B.s still exist? Sooner or later they will have all disappeared and there will be no more

Sons of the battlefield of Bitche left in this world. May their children and their children's children have the wisdom to keep these strange identification cards which someday will be a precious collector's item.

As for me, if someday my many years of work with the United Nations should gain me the gratitude of my people, nothing would please me more than to be honored by that town as a "Son of Bitche" for peace and to receive a memorable certificate to that effect!

23

The Cross of Hambach

The world has become beautifully small.

December 1959. The UN Economic Commission for Africa had just been created and was holding one of its first sessions in Tangiers, Morocco. I accompanied the UN Under-Secretary-General for economic and social affairs to it. Dag Hammarskjöld was also present. He was deeply concerned about Africa, the last continent on earth to become independent at a time in history when there existed a first world organization. In his view, it was the historical role of the United Nations to help Africa gain its independence with a minimum of bloodshed and to keep it insulated from the world's big powers. He knew how tempting it was for foreign nations to intervene, subvert, foment troubles and secessions, and transform African independence into a chaos in order to keep or gain influence. He was determined to have the UN play a primary peace-keeping role in that region during his mandate.

In Tangiers this hammarskjöldian strategy became quite obvious.

His speech to the Economic Commission for Africa has remained a classic on Africa's future. He called a meeting of some of his collaborators to form a mission to several West African countries on the eve of their independence. The purpose of the mission was to offer them United Nations technical assistance, but no less important in Hammar-

skjöld's mind was the desire to have a UN presence in these
countries in case political trouble broke out. The team was
composed of David Owen, Chairman of the UN Technical
Assistance Board, Wilfred Benson, UN Resident Representative in Ghana, and myself.

From among the many anecdotes of that fascinating
trip, which took us from the region of veiled women in the
north to that of naked women in the tropics, from deserts to
steaming forests, from English-speaking to French-speak-
ing countries, from left-hand- to right-hand-driving lands, I
will narrate one anecdote that took place in Nigeria.

The United Nations had already established a small
nucleus of personnel in that country before its independence in 1960: UNICEF was helping Nigerian children, the
World Health Organization had programs for malaria eradi-
cation and leprosy control, the World Bank had sent a mission to survey the economic potential of the country, and
the International Labor Office had appointed a regional
representative for West Africa in Lagos. This office was to
become later the first UN Representative's office in Nigeria,
a matter we had come to discuss with the Nigerian preinde-
pendence authorities. I remember very well the little building in which it was located, in Ikoye, the white residential
area. From its windows one could see a large cemetery.
Curious as always, I asked my Nigerian driver what the
beautifully sounding word Ikoye meant, and he answered:
"Cemetery!" When later I asked my ILO colleague the
same question, he could not answer. Pointing at the vast
field of tombs, I told him:

"It means cemetery. The British and the whites are
living on a graveyard. Isn't that symbolic?"

The official in question, Mr. Morizot, was a French compatriot. He invited me for dinner at his home. During the
evening, he asked me where I came from in France and I

told him that I was from a town called Sarreguemines right on the border with Germany. Whereupon he commented:

"I was an officer in that region during World War II and perhaps you might be able to clarify a point which has always remained a mystery to me. Do you know by any chance a village called Hambach?"

"Yes, I know it very well indeed. It is located between my hometown and the village of Sarralbe, where my grandparents lived. I crossed and visited it innumerable times."

"Well, I commanded an artillery unit during the war and I was ordered to establish my headquarters in that village. What struck me most when I arrived were the manure heaps located in front of every house. I wondered how people could live with such odors right outside of their homes."

"The reason is very simple: as distinct from Alsace, which is a flat and spacious land, that part of Lorraine is very hilly and the villages are built in the form of elongated strings of houses on both sides of a main road, usually an ancient postroad, winding through small elevations. The ancient counts and princes levied a tax on the number of doors and windows on the front of the houses from which people could watch the road. As a result, in order to avoid the tax, the peasants decided to locate their kitchens and bedrooms in the back and to put the manure heaps in front of the houses! This is the origin of the peculiar appearance of the Lorraine villages."

"Well, I found that the only house without a manure heap was the priest's parish house next to the church. It was empty like all other dwellings, since the village had been evacuated. Do you remember that parish house?"

"Yes, I remember it very well. It was all covered with ivy, and it had a very romantic appearance. It made me sometimes dream of becoming a priest, for I thought that it must be wonderful to live in such a charming place, to be its spiritual leader, to know an entire human community, its virtues and its sins, its births and its deaths, its joys and its sorrows, and its uniqueness in the universe."

The former officer commented: "In reality the house was rather small and there was no room in which I could hold staff meetings and spread out my artillery maps. I decided, therefore, to merge two rooms by pulling down a wall. When the soldiers did the job they uncovered . . . a secret safe in the wall! We blew it open and found in it a large quantity of documents and correspondence, all in German. I do not know German but I could well notice that most letters ended with 'Heil Hitler.' I therefore sent the entire material to French counterespionage. I never heard anything from them, and I have often wondered why there was a hidden safe in that wall, what these German letters meant and who was the strange priest of that parish. Do you know anything about him?"

"Yes, but nothing very conclusive. His name was Abbé Pink. He was a very intelligent and learned man who did much to collect and save from oblivion the legends and customs of the rural areas of Lorraine. He published many historical and cultural articles. He was helped in this task by his sister, who directed in Frankfurt-am-Main in Germany an Alsace-Lorraine institute. When the Germans occupied our region, they tried very hard to enlist him in their efforts and to have him take publicly a position for Hitler, but without avail. He died during the war and I remember that the Nazis organized a pompous official funeral for him in the village, with martial speeches, a big display of flags and the participation of many Nazi organizations. According to local belief, his heart was not on the Nazi side but with the people of Lorraine. It is said that he even helped some young men to hide and escape from the German army. This is all I know."

My host remained silent for a while. Then he called his maid, a Greek girl, and said to her:

"Maria, could you go to your room and bring the cross which hangs on the wall beside your bed."

She returned with an enameled cross, the size of the palm of a hand. It was not a precious object, but one of those multicolored enamel works which one can buy in religious stores. The city of Nancy in Lorraine is reputed for such crosses. It must have had only a sentimental value to its owner.

He handed it to me and said:

"I found this cross in the safe. I kept it as a war souvenir. It has accompanied me ever since."

I held the cross for a long while in my hand. We were silent. Outdoors the heavy tropical night had fallen. Ventilators were gently mixing the hot, humid air. Crickets were chirping in multitudes. My thoughts were far from Lagos. They were in the little village of Hambach where they saw a church, an empty parish, abandoned homes, French troops, a wall being torn down, a safe, documents, a funeral, and books of legends of my homeland. I wondered what strange fate had brought me here, to faraway Africa, trying to prepare the ground for a better, more peaceful, more gentle world, and holding in my hands the cross of Abbé Pink! The world had become very small indeed. Nothing can be hidden anymore. Every act has a consequence. Perhaps as a result of the exiguity of our planet, for the first time ever in evolution, it will be possible for humans to live together in peace and friendship. It was our only way to survive. The little cross of Hambach suddenly acquired for me a deeply moving and unforgettable significance. I prayed to it silently to bless the United Nations and all world servants who like me are entrusted with the task of peacemaking and friendship-building on this planet.

24

A Point of History

When will humans learn once and for all to live in peace and to administer their planet well instead of getting involved in nonsensical wars, revolutions and violence?

September 1975. I had been invited to address the annual meeting of the International Association of Business Communicators in New Orleans. My wife and I had never visited that beautiful city, world-known for its moving and well-preserved past. New Orleans held its promise beyond all our expectations. We found a city with a soul, a past, a story, a continuity, where one likes to stroll, to muse and to enjoy the endless spectacles of life. For there is always something new to see in New Orleans that captivates the heart, the mind or the imagination: an old courtyard, an ancient object in one of the countless antique shops, a beautiful restoration, not to speak of the magnificent ironworks which give the old French quarter an absolutely unique cachet in the world. This is a city worth living in and loving, unlike so many American cities which look alike, whose history has been destroyed and whose old centers have been bulldozed, pulverized and replaced by the same unappealing, monotonous skyscrapers which nowhere but in New York—their natural birthplace—possess a real soul or grandeur. To stand and muse on the old square in front of St. Louis Cathedral, flanked on both sides by two Spanish wings of buildings opening their arms to the incoming ships, is quite a moving experience. Here one can sit on a bench among painters and vendors and dream serenely about the past lives, sufferings, hopes and joys which inhabited human brothers and sisters long ago on this tiny spot of earth. Museums and carefully restored homes tell you exactly how people lived here in the olden days. One is given a sense of continuity and time, an image of the human journey on our little planet, and hence a feeling of inner peace, of belonging to something which reaches far beyond the transience of our brief individual lives. Yes, here in New Orleans, one can feel the heartbeat of human history.

We arrived in the city on a Friday evening and thus had an entire weekend to ourselves. Thereafter I had mostly to attend meetings, while my wife pursued her exploration of the city and of its surroundings. On the fourth and last day I was free again and my wife became my experienced guide. It was then that in a bookstore I found a collection of volumes which became one of my most cherished possessions: an original illustrated edition of Chateaubriand's works sold more than a hundred years ago in an old New Orleans bookstore, the Librairie Hébert, at a time when Chateaubriand was still alive. As a boy in my faraway Lorraine I read with tears in my eyes the touching love story of Atala, the American Indian maid, and the moving description of the Meschacebe or Mississippi River by my preferred author.[1] I would have never dared to dream that some day in my life I would stand on the banks of that river and hold in my hands and read aloud a book which had traveled across the Atlantic during the life of the author to bring joy and solace to French settlers in the sweet province of Louisiana, or Nouvelle France. The collection is not com-

---

[1] I loved it so much that I later wrote a similar book unfolding in India: *Sima, mon amour.*

plete, but I am endlessly delighted to possess it, to touch its venerable bindings, to peruse its beautiful engravings and to read the same old romantic passages which transported me to heaven when I was an adolescent. On the same day, in a museum near the cathedral, we met a French family from Grenoble who had come especially to Louisiana to retrace the life and steps of an ancestor whose voluminous correspondence with the homeland, filled with descriptions and historical details, they had just found in an old family trunk in France.

But most important, it was in New Orleans that I came across a piece of historical information concerning World War II in Lorraine. As we strolled through the town, my wife drew my attention to an antique store where she had bought some objects the previous day and whose owner had treated her very well.

We entered the shop which was packed with collections of old things for any conceivable purpose and taste. A man was busy in a workshop adjacent to the store. After we had browsed around and made some selections, he came to the counter to wrap our purchases. We talked a little. I noticed that he had a German accent and I asked him where he came from. He answered: "From Stuttgart in Germany." When I told him that I came from neighboring Alsace-Lorraine in France, he asked me if I knew a city called Metz.

"Of course! Extremely well. During the evacuation of my hometown in 1939–40, we lived for some time in Metz, where I went to high school."

He continued:

"I was stationed in Metz during the entire war, from 1940 to the defeat of Germany. I was a pilot in a squadron stationed at Frescati, the airport of Metz. I was a young volunteer. My first plane was a Stuka. Do you remember the Stukas?"

"Do I remember them! When they attacked Metz for the first time, in May 1940, I was one of the spectators in the streets. We applauded when we saw the German planes fall down. But to our dismay we then saw them shoot up again after having dropped their bombs. We could not understand what was going on. We had never seen such planes. Hitler had kept them a great secret. The whole operation lasted only a half-hour. Every single French airplane on the ground was destroyed."

"Yes. I was the pilot of one of those Stukas. We took possession of the airport soon thereafter when the German troops entered Metz. I stayed there for the rest of the war and participated mostly in actions against American and English bombers who were flying into Germany. Frescati was bombed several times. Once, after a heavy air combat, I wanted to land, when I saw the airport covered with bomb craters, resembling a Swiss cheese. I used up as much gasoline as I could and finally landed with the nose of my plane stuck in one of those holes! By miracle I escaped unharmed. I was born in 1923 and was then a very young man. Hitler's propaganda was very effective. It went to my head and I volunteered for the air force. Today I have all the difficulties in the world to explain to my American son that I was not an infamous Nazi but that the German youth sincerely believed in Hitler, admired him and thought that he would bring good to our people and to the world. I would lie to my son if I denied today that I loved Hitler, that he was my hero as he was for the entire German youth, that we were galvanized by him and ready to die for him. My son hates me for saying that, but it was the truth. I wish you could talk to him and explain how it was."

After a long silence, I asked him:

"What did you do when the Germans hurriedly abandoned Lorraine in November 1944, believing that Patton's army would move in, but instead the Americans remained stuck in Nancy for lack of fuel? It was rumored at the time that Gauleiter Bürckel had to commit suicide or was shot on the orders of Hitler for his blunder. It was then that my father was released from prison. Someone had called the various jails in Lorraine and ordered on behalf of the gauleiter that all inmates be released forthwith in view of the American advance. Later on the Nazis discovered that it was a hoax."

"Well, I can fill in a point of history for you in this respect. The commander of our air base was also afraid that the Americans would move in quickly. Metz was only an hour away by tank from Nancy. He didn't have enough pilots to take the planes to Germany. He decided therefore to blow up the best planes to prevent them from falling into American hands and kept only a few older machines. Then it became apparent that the Americans were stalled and that the German troops had panicked. One morning the meager personnel left at the airport was asked to line up on the field. A plane landed. Out of it stepped Adolf Hitler in person, accompanied by several aides. He addressed us in a harsh, vociferous voice, accusing us of having panicked in the most shameful way. I was standing very close to him. It was quite an extraordinary event for me to see for the first time the Führer in person. He soon withdrew with the officers. A quick court-martial was held and our commanding officer was condemned and shot. When the group was about to leave, an aide asked me if there was a hospital nearby. The Führer was sick, very sick. He looked livid and green, as if in a state of utter shock. In my opinion, he had taken drugs! This came to me as a total surprise. I was frankly disappointed by the man. I would have never imagined Hitler as a drug addict. This was so far from the ideal of a pure Aryan life he was preaching us!"

Astonished by what I had learned, I commented:

"Up to this day I had never heard any account of a personal visit of Hitler to Metz at that time."

"It took place in great secret. The whole affair lasted less than an hour. We were very few people left at the airport."

I looked at the man standing in front of me. We were exactly the same age, having both been born in 1923. I asked him if he sometimes returned to Germany and if he still liked the old country. He said:

"Yes. I return to Stuttgart every year with my family. When my mother died last year, I found a box containing all the letters I had written to her during the war from Metz. As a result, I even have the exact dates of such events. I like America very much, especially New Orleans. I would not wish to live anywhere else. Here in this city I feel at home. It is like living in a European town as they were during my youth. New Orleans is such a warm and civilized city."

We said good-bye to each other, hoping that we would meet again someday. I invited him to pay me a visit at the United Nations if he ever came to New York.

On the plane back to New York I held pensively in my hands one of the precious volumes of Chateaubriand and I read the beloved romantic passages describing the Mississippi River:

> In its course of more than a thousand leagues, the river waters a delightful region which the inhabitants of the United States call New Eden and to which our countrymen have given the gentle name of Louisiana . . . When storms have blown down whole patches of forest, the streams become blocked with uprooted trees. These are quickly bound together by creepers, and plants root everywhere in the mud which gradually cements

them into single masses . . . The river takes
hold of them, carries them down to the Mexi-
can gulf, runs them aground on sandbanks and
thus multiplies the number of its estuaries.
Now and again, thundering between steep
banks, its waters overflow and spread about
the forest colonnades and the pyramid tombs
of the Indians; it is a Nile of the wilderness. But
in these scenes of nature, grace and magnifi-
cence go together: while the main current
drags the dead pines and oaks to the sea, floating islands of lotus and water-lilies, their yellow blooms raised like standards, are borne
upstream along both banks. Green snakes,
blue herons, red flamingoes, and young croco-
diles travel as passengers on these flowering
boats, and each colony, spreading its golden
sails to the wind, will come to rest in its own
quiet backwater . . .[2]

I let the book rest on my lap and began to dream. I saw
my room in my hometown of Sarreguemines where I read
Chateaubriand on the eve of World War II. I saw my father's
playmate from Sarralbe, who became a German spy and the
Vice-Gauleiter of Lorraine. I saw the young German in his
Stuka falling like a stone from the sky. I saw images of war
and indescribable violence. And I saw the tall United Nations building in New York jutting like a prayer of blue glass
and marble into the sky, embodying humanity's still unfulfilled dreams for peace and happiness. Fate had brought me
there to work for a better world. Fate had now brought me
to New Orleans to learn thirty-one years later that Hitler

[2] *Atala*, by François de Chateaubriand.

had come to Metz to have the commander of the German
air base shot, as well as probably Gauleiter Bürckel. Today
the Vice-Gauleiter and German spy is in Latin America. His
son is in Asia. The Stuka pilot is in New Orleans and I am in
the United Nations! What a strange planet is ours! How
people are mixed all over its surface today. I would never
come to the end of my surprises. I asked myself the question: when will humans learn once and for all to live in
peace, to stay at home, to administer their planet well and
no longer to get involved in nonsensical wars, revolutions
and violence? A warm feeling of comfort and joy overcame
me when I thought that after the long and atrocious World
War II, I had been allowed to devote my entire adult life to a
first serious worldwide effort toward permanent peace and
brotherhood on this planet. Perhaps after all the human
race was not so bad. There was a lot of reasonable hope for
its success and further ascent. Perhaps the time was near
when we would be able to live forever without any new
world war. What more could I do to help achieve that objective? Work harder. Never give up. And perhaps, after a
lifetime of world service, write down for a wider audience
and for future generations the fascinating story of my life,
work, efforts, dreams, hopes, satisfactions and disappointments in the first universal temple of the new global, planetary age: the United Nations. May God fulfill this last dream
of mine, so that the youth which will follow will benefit
from our experience and take humanity a step further on its
way to world peace, cooperation and happiness on our beloved and so incredibly beautiful planet in the universe.

25

Conclusions and Proposals

What are the conclusions I have drawn from these war-related experiences?

They have left a deep mark on me and have stayed with me to the present day in my work at the United Nations. I mention them, never tiring, in my speeches on world affairs and the United Nations. In order to remind myself of these experiences and of my pledge to work relentlessly for peace and for a better world, I keep always within sight in my office a few of the rare memorabilia from that period of my life. The principal lessons I have drawn are the following:

1. I am convinced today more than ever of the sacrosanct, divine character of human life and of our planet. My attitude toward them has not changed since I was a child. Yes, life is *göttlich* (divine). Yes, our planet is the Planet of God. Yes, we are the children of God. If humanity has failed so far in its peace efforts, it is primarily because we have not recognized the supreme sanctity of human life, the divine character of our planet and the tremendous value they represent in the universe. We continue to fail because all kinds of secondary, limited objectives, groups or geographical areas are erected as the supreme values, and this, unavoidably, leads to divisions, wars and conflicts. Humanity as a

whole and the preservation of our planet must become the paramount concerns of our time and of all peoples. Once this is done—and it will inexorably be done because no one can stop evolution—everything will at long last fall into place.

2. I have often asked myself the question, as I did when I was a young boy: "Why do they do this to me? What right have governments and leaders to interfere in the peaceful course of my life and my family's life? What right do they have to endanger all human life and the entire planet with their horrid weapons? What right do they have to ask me to kill a human brother and to risk my life for their political aims?" I have therefore come to the conclusion that it is high time for the people to request the sacred right "not to kill and not to be killed, not even in the name of a nation." Our leaders should never have the right to resort to war in order to settle their differences. There are plenty of other means, which are all spelled out in the United Nations Charter, to which all member-governments of this planet have pledged solemn allegiance. We must establish an entirely new set of global human rights, including the right to a peaceful, disarmed, safe and well-preserved planet. States must be deprived of the right to kill, to arm themselves and to endanger the planet under the pretext of good government.

3. I have been fully exposed to the hypocrisy of national objectives because I and my family were told time and again that this or that nation was the greatest, and then the next occupants came and told us that *they* were the greatest and that the others had lied to us. And in each case they put hatred into our hearts, violence into our heads and guns into our hands. No wonder that you cease to believe in such games when they are repeated

so often. The only way out is to elevate yourself and to
see what two nations and all nations have in common,
namely the fact of being composed of humans. This is
why a borderland like Alsace-Lorraine has produced an
Erwin von Steinbach, builder of cathedrals, a Meister
Eckhart, the great humanists of the Rhine Valley, an
Albert Schweitzer and a Robert Schuman, the father of
Europe.[1] This is why it has inspired to world humanism
a man like Goethe and has sent flocks of its sons and
daughters to the first European and world organizations. This is why Strasbourg was selected as the seat of
the Council of Europe. As Norman Cousins once told
me: "Robert, you cannot be different from what you
are, because of your origins: what happened to Albert
Schweitzer is also happening to you."

4. Hence my impassioned belief in the United Nations,
the first chance ever given to humanity as the supreme
family and to the planet as our common home. Of
course, it is an imperfect organization, unworthy of the
plenitude of the human genius, but at least we have it,
we can nurture it, love it, strengthen it, support it and
transform it into a momentous, unprecedented instrument for peace and a better world. My heart bleeds and
my reason protests when I see people—blinded by their
group allegiance—throw stones at their best chance
ever for peace and human unity. I address therefore
this appeal to all my human brothers and sisters on this
planet: learn about the UN, take an interest in the UN,
love the UN, understand the UN, support the UN and
force your government to abide by its charter and to

[1] Perhaps Robert Schuman should appear last in the film suggested in
footnote 3 of Chapter 2. He would bring a note of hope and forward vision
as a climax.

make it work. I beg you: please do not listen to the
eternal negativists, pessimists and tenents of darkness
and hopelessness. Do not believe that peace is impossible. Do not believe that justice is impossible. Do not
believe that disarmament is impossible. On the contrary, believe with all your heart that peace is possible,
that a disarmed planet is possible, that world justice is
possible, that truth and love are possible, that human
cooperation and world government are possible. All
belief starts with you and me. What we believe will be.

5. Do not blame the UN for the present state of the world.
    Blame the nations which do not abide by its rules and
    which pay only lip service to it. World War II was not
    caused by the League of Nations. It was caused by the
    nonmembership of the United States in that organiza-
    tion, by the betrayal of Japan, Italy and Germany, and
    by irresponsible games of nations. When the League
    died, the delegates in their departing speeches belat-
    edly recognized that the League had been too much
    taken for granted and had not been supported by mem-
    ber-governments as it should have been! May this mis-
    take never again be repeated as regards the United
    Nations.

6. I would advise patience and perseverance. It is just
    impossible to solve all the deep-seated colossal prob-
    lems of humanity and of this planet over a short period
    of forty years. On some we have done very well: the
    eradication of all major epidemics, feeding 2 billion
    more people, an unprecedented increase of longevity,
    decolonization, greater racial equality, greater equality
    between men and women, nine tenths of the nations of
    this planet now living in peace, etc. On others we have
    done poorly, in particular armaments, which are worse
    today than ever. But the last thing to do would be to

give up. I just do not believe that billions of years of evolution have as their sole purpose a blowing up of this planet and a nuclear holocaust of the human species. It just cannot be. We must on the contrary use the nuclear stalemate to develop understanding and cooperation in every conceivable field, not leaving a single stone unturned. "What can I do?" you will ask me. Well, as a mother you can raise peaceful and understanding children. Perhaps tomorrow one of them will be the President of your country. As a doctor you can cooperate with doctors all around the world. There are today tens of thousands of international private professional associations covering every conceivable field. Join yours, thereby promoting world understanding and cooperation.

7. We must continue to elevate ourselves, to dream, to visualize in our mind a better future, a peaceful, just, loving, kind and beautiful planet, and conceive proper political relations, communications and world structures for our magnificent abode in the universe. We do not dream enough, we do not plan enough, we do not believe enough, we do not cooperate enough, we do not inspire each other enough for the further ascent of the human race. We need infinitely more Meister Eckharts, Albert Schweitzers and Robert Schumans. We need bold, new plans and values for our world, like those which Jean Monnet dreamed of, promoted and implemented in Europe. We need again great universal minds, hearts, dreamers and believers like Woodrow Wilson and Franklin Roosevelt at the helm of governments. Let us pray to God that some will soon reappear on this planet.

8. When I joined the United Nations in 1948, I was a very pessimistic young man. The horrors, killings and hatred

I saw between France and Germany, two very civilized countries, located in Europe and which had waged three wars during my grandfather's lifetime, had made me doubt of the human species. If things could not work out between these two neighboring countries, how could they ever work out between such distant cultures as Russia, the United States, China and so many others, between black and white, rich and poor, north and south, capitalism and communism, religion and atheism, in the midst of frightful atomic weaponry? As a result, at the age of twenty-five, when I set foot in Lake Success, the first seat of the United Nations, I was convinced that within twenty years there would be another world war. It seemed unavoidable. The problems were too immense to give us a chance. At that time, most Alsace-Lorrainers who lived in Manhattan moved to the north of the state of New York in order to be away from an atomic attack on the city. Today, at the age of sixty-two, I am astonished to be still alive and that there has not been another world war! It seems incredible to me. This is why I have become an optimist. Yes, this planet is in bad political shape and is administered appallingly. An outer-space inspection team would undoubtedly give us an F (failure) or a triple D (dumb, deficient and dangerous) in planetary management. Our world is afflicted by a good dozen conflicts almost permanently. Its skies, lands and oceans are infested with atomic weapons which cost humanity 850 billion dollars a year, while so many poor people are still dying of hunger on this planet. And yet, I have seen the UN become universal and prevent many conflicts. I have seen the dangerous decolonization[2] page turned

[2] In 1948, when I joined the UN, the feeling of the Secretariat was that decolonization would take from one hundred to one hundred fifty

quickly and with infinitely less bloodshed than in Europe and the Americas in preceding centuries. I have seen a flowering expansion of international cooperation in thirty-two UN specialized agencies and world programs. I have seen the birth of world conferences and international years concerned with practically every field of human endeavor, from outer space to the atom, from the atmosphere to the depths of the oceans, from the mountains to the deserts, from the polar caps to the tropics, from world population to individual human rights, from the preservation of the past to planning for the future. Being in charge of the coordination of this colossal work, I became known as the "optimist-in-residence" at the UN, an epithet of which I am rather proud. I believe indeed that if we reduce the lies and political nonsense on this planet, if we continue to increase vigorously international cooperation, we will have a good chance to make it past the year 2000 and to enter at long last an era of permanent peace and proper planetary management in the next century. I believe this on the strength of what I have observed during the last thirty-seven years in the United Nations. May God and the future bear me out.

9. I believe that the greatest defect and defeat for an individual is to do nothing and to wait and wail until the world has improved. This is in my view the greatest trouble on this planet. There is a formidable strength in the 4.5 billion people of this earth. The power of the people is immense if they care to exercise it. Each individual from morning to evening throughout an entire life can be a factor for peace, an agent of love, truth,

---

years. It took less than forty years. Perhaps on other world issues we might be similarly overpessimistic today.

cooperation and kindness. No leader of this world can be insensitive to the power of the people. None of them can send his or her people into killing if they refuse in the name of humanity and God. How can we expect a peaceful, nonviolent world if it does not start with the individual? I cannot change 4.5 billion people, but I can change myself. If many people begin to be less violent, to speak better about others, to tell the truth, to be more understanding, to cooperate, then we will have a better world. My advice to my 4.5 billion brothers and sisters on this planet is therefore to be each an instrument of the peace of God, to be an active, relentless, passionate, enthusiastic, inspired agent for the success of the tremendous cosmic, divine, human destiny and evolution unfolding on this planet in the vast universe. Shall the people of peace lie on their backs and remain silent and idle while our misguided military brothers fill the airs, the oceans, the soils and the heavens with their abominable weapons? Shall we forever accept their alleged imperative reasons for doing it when we know perfectly that tomorrow they will find another reason, and after that yet another, as they have done for thousands of years, always at the expense of the poor and the downtrodden. Therefore my advice would be:

Decide to be peaceful
Render others peaceful
Be a model of peace
Irradiate your peace
Love passionately the peace
    of our beautiful planet
Do not listen to the warmongers,
    hateseeders and powerseekers
Dream always of a peaceful,
    warless, disarmed world
Think always of a peaceful world
Work always for a peaceful world
Switch on and keep on, in yourself,
    the peaceful buttons,
    those marked love,
    serenity, happiness, truth,
    kindness, friendliness,
    understanding and tolerance
Pray and thank God every day for peace
Pray for the United Nations
    and all peacemakers
Pray for the leaders of nations
    who hold the peace of the world
    in their hands
Pray God to let our planet at long last
    become the Planet of Peace
And sing in unison with all humanity:

    "Let there be peace on Earth
And let it begin with me."

I finished writing these anecdotes and conclusions in December 1983, at Christmastime. It was to be my last year at the United Nations. My retirement was due in March 1984. My dear wife was asking me: "What are your plans? What will we do? Will we remain here in the United States or return to France? You are still young. Will you take up another job? For instance, you could teach young people about the UN in a university?" I answered her: "I do not know. I leave it to God who knows much better than I what is good for me. I would not dare to interfere in His plans with my will."

Early in February, the Secretary-General, Mr. Javier Pérez de Cuéllar, called me to his office and said to me:

"There are two officials in this house whom I would hate to see leave: one is Brian Urquhart[3] and the other is you. If you are prepared to stay, I would be happy to relieve you of your administrative duties and put you in charge of the preparations of the fortieth anniversary of the United Nations in 1985. You will not stand in the way of younger colleagues. You would occupy an additional, temporary post financed by a voluntary contribution of the government of Japan."

I accepted forthwith, thanking him, God and Japan for a wonderful idea which I would have been unable to conceive myself. The story of this last assignment at the UN and my conclusions after thirty-seven years of world service will require further thought and writing after my retirement.

[3.] Brian Urquhart, Under-Secretary-General for Special Political Affairs, has the longest record of service with the United Nations: forty years. He started to work for the UN as one of its first officials at Church House in London. He too had plenty of adventures during World War II, including a fall with an unopened parachute! He too is a lucid fanatic of the United Nations, endlessly serving, speaking, writing and trying to convince the public to support the UN, and governments to abide by the charter. He is lovingly called "The Last of the Mohicans" of the United Nations.

Months later, shortly before Christmas, the General Assembly of the UN adopted a unanimous resolution which calls essentially for:

I. an unprecedented commemoration and solemn recommitment to the UN and the charter on the fortieth anniversary of the world body on 24 October 1985, attended by as many heads of state as possible from all around the planet;

II. unprecedented worldwide thinking on the human condition and planning for a better world by the year 2000, the motto of the commemoration being "United Nations for a Better World";

III. the creation of national committees to that effect and the holding of national commemorations in each country;

IV. the request to governments that both children and adults be better educated about the work, aims and achievements of the United Nations;

V. several other recommendations of a similar nature addressed to international agencies, nongovernmental organizations, the media and the people.

The General Assembly had adjourned, the framework for the commemoration was laid out, the preparations were well underway. I was happy and relaxed, enjoying the warmth of Christmas and of a year-end family reunion with all our children and our first grandchild. Then in my mail I found the announcement of an essay contest by the *Christian Science Monitor* that someone had sent me. It asked "future historians" to write from the point of view of the year 2010 about how lasting peace had come to be established during the last twenty-five years, i.e., from the year

1985. There were only three days left to submit the essay, the deadline being 31 December.

Remembering the essay on a world government which opened the doors of the United Nations to me when I was a young man after World War II, I considered this to be a direct challenge to me, thirty-seven years later, at the end of my career. I sat down and wrote the following essay, dreaming that the United States and the U.S.S.R. would work together as was foreseen by the founding fathers of the UN. Who knows? Since two arch-enemies like France and Germany could finally make peace and work together for the good of my homeland and of Europe, perhaps God might inspire the leaders of the U.S. and of the U.S.S.R. to change course and to work together for the good of the world. Is it so inconceivable to dream that this might happen during the last fifteen years of this millennium? So help us God.

Here is this essay, which may fittingly conclude this book and, I hope, help open a new chapter in human history.

PEACE 2010

Christian Science Monitor, year 2010

24 October 2010. The world celebrates the sixty-fifth anniversary of the United Nations, its sixty-fifth year without a world war and its tenth year of total peace, without a single conflict to report. As is now the practice, the media publish each year, on UN Day, articles on what has been accomplished and on what remains to be done. This article recapitulates how world peace was achieved during the last twenty-five years.

1985

1. Fortieth anniversary of the UN. Forty years of cold war. A dozen out of 159 nations are still engaged in local wars. A deep-freeze in U.S./U.S.S.R. relations. An upsurge of nuclear armaments. A risk of spread of nuclear armaments to outer space. East/West and North/South talks and cooperation at a standstill. The Secretary-General of the UN declares the world in chaos and calls for an urgent change in course on the occasion of the fortieth anniversary of the UN.

2. 26 June 1985: At the invitation of the President of the United States the heads of state of the permanent members of the Security Council (China, France, United Kingdom, the U.S. and U.S.S.R.) meet in San Francisco to commemorate the signing of the UN Charter in that city, to rededicate themselves to the charter and to embark upon a new planetary deal to achieve world peace by the year 2000 and disarmament by 2010.

3. 24 October 1985: General meeting of heads of state at the UN to renew their commitment to the charter and to plan a new course for humanity. The Secretary-General reports to the General Assembly on accomplishments and failures during the first forty years of the UN:

    On the plus side: decolonization practically accomplished; trusteeship chapter of the charter can be closed; UN has become universal; unprecedented legal regimes have been adopted for the world's commons (the seas and oceans and outer space); human rights charters adopted for all groups of people; thirty-two specialized agencies and world programs were created to deal with practically every facet of our planet and of humanity's condition; world statistics, data and yearly diagnostics now available on all major world issues;

global warnings effectively given through a series of resounding world conferences and international years; pendulums of world population increase and of environmental deterioration slowing down; demands of the poor, of women, of races, of children, of the elderly, of the handicapped all brought to the world forum, followed by national and international action; peace is now the expected norm on the planet rather than war.

On the minus side: armaments infinitely worse than in 1945; too many unresolved conflicts, some of them more than twenty years old; 500 million hungry in the world; 12 million refugees; African continent a disaster area as a result of climatic changes; 850 billion dollars squandered each year on armaments; little progress if any in world democracy; recent attempts to weaken the UN and its agencies instead of strengthening them boldly in the face of emerging global problems and world interdependence.

4. General Assembly adopts a turning-point declaration and requests the Secretary-General, in consultation with governments and the best minds of this planet, to prepare a fifteen-year plan for world peace by the year 2000 and total disarmament by the year 2010. All member-governments are requested to submit their proposals. National committees are established with people's participation for the formulation of ideas and practical steps toward "Peace 2000, Disarmament 2010." General Assembly asks that all existing UN plans 2000 (Food 2000, Health 2000, Literacy 2000, Industry 2000, Employment 2000, Population 2000, Environment 2000, Telecommunications 2000 and the Economic development decades) be put together into a World 2000 Action Plan. The General Assembly also takes note of the first positive achievements toward Peace 2000: the set-

tlement of the Beagle Channel dispute between Argentina and Chile; the agreement between the United Kingdom and the People's Republic of China for the transfer of Hong Kong by 1997; the implementation of the Panama Canal settlement on 31 December 1999. The General Assembly calls for a momentous acceleration of similar settlements of all conflicts and disputes in order for humanity to enter the next millennium with a clean slate.

1986

5. On the basis of governmental proposals and the Fifteen-Year Peace Plan of the Secretary-General, the following Twelve World Steps were set into motion during 1986 (International Year of Peace):

   I. Security Council to meet at least once a year at the head-of-state level to make decisions, settle disputes, finalize agreements and give instructions for further action. Council to meet in various parts of the world, including in trouble spots.

   II. Summit meetings of Eastern, Western and Nonaligned countries capped by a yearly summit meeting of all nations during the General Assembly.

   III. Bilateral visits of heads of state, especially of U.S. and U.S.S.R., fostered. Yearly reports on such visits to General Assembly.

   IV. A world conference on security is decided on for 1988, to remain in session like the Law of the Sea Conference until it has produced a world security system.

V. Establishment of a United Nations force as required by the UN Charter to render enforceable and effective the decisions of the Security Council.

VI. Revival and considerable strengthening of the Military Staff Committee of the charter, with the tasks of: 1. planning the creation of the World Disarmament Agency foreseen in the McCloy-Zorin agreement; 2. reviewing and adopting measures to prevent a nuclear war by accident; 3. planning military cooperation in multiple fields, including the creation of a UN fleet to control the seas and oceans and of a UN satellite system to control disarmament as proposed by France.

VII. Preparation of a Marshall or Manhattan Plan for massive help to the poor countries, hand in hand with savings from disarmament in rich and in poor countries. Implementation of a series of major world engineering, power and development projects to increase dramatically the overall productivity of the world economy.

VIII. Fostering of nuclear free zones and neutral nonarmed countries guaranteed by UN forces.

IX. Setting up of high-technology direct communication, video and teleconferencing systems between the heads of states of the members of the Security Council, especially the permanent members and the Secretary-General.

X. Bold strengthening of the Secretary-General's office for conflict prevention. Establishment of a high-technology Peace Room for the Secretary-

General and the Security Council to forestall, track, contain and solve conflicts.

XI. All UN agencies and world programs requested to revive major plans and projects for world cooperation which had been shelved as a result of the Cold War. Concept of risk capital to be applied to world cooperation, which requires bold, new approaches commensurate with the magnitude of the world's global problems and growing interdependence.

XII. Establishment of Peace Ministries, Peace Academies or Peace Universities in all countries.

6. All the above steps to be implemented at the latest by the year 1995, fiftieth anniversary of the UN.

1986–2000

7. By 1988, the Economic and Social Council of the UN had drafted a Marshall Plan for the dramatic improvement of the standards of living of the poor countries, the pump-priming of the world economy and a plan for major world development and engineering projects.

8. By 1995, the UN Conference on World Security had completed its work and adopted a treaty for ratification by member-governments within a year.

9. The Military Staff Committee completed its work on the prevention of nuclear accidents by 1988, on a UN satellite system for disarmament control and on a UN fleet by 1990, and on the detailed blueprints for a World Disarmament Agency by 1995.

10. The remaining Twelve World Steps were implemented by 1995, creating a good deal of enthusiasm, emulation and stimulation among governments, which were now

convinced that world peace was possible, if taken seriously, with all necessary precaution and without undue haste.

11. The entire period 1986–2000 was characterized by an unprecedented flourishing of ideas, activities and achievements, toward the advent in 2000 of a new planetary age. Here are a few examples:

    I. In 1987, the bicentennial of the U.S. Constitution, the U.S. appointed a group of eminent jurists to draft a World Constitution, which was proposed to all nations in 1992 on the occasion of the 500th anniversary of the discovery of the New World. It contained provisions for world democracy, world elections and world public opinion polls, all rendered possible by the computer age.

    II. Costa Rica had its borders and unarmed neutrality guaranteed by UN forces from neutral countries. Several other countries followed its example and received premium international economic assistance as a result of their disarmament.

    III. The U.S. and U.S.S.R. agreed to tone down their claims of total righteousness and to have the respective achievements of their systems studied and evaluated objectively in the United Nations and in a U.S./U.S.S.R. joint institute for the study of socialism and of the free enterprise system.

    IV. The U.S. and U.S.S.R. similarly agreed that the concept and practice of freedom be studied and evaluated throughout the UN system and in the joint U.S./U.S.S.R. institute for the study of socialism and the free enterprise system.

V. A World Cadastre of property registration was established in order to determine what exactly the legal status of ownership was in the present world: the world commons (outer space and the seas and oceans beyond the limits of national jurisdiction), national and state property, municipal properties, corporate properties, religious and private associations' ownership and individual ownership.

VI. Following the example of the world navigation satellite of the UN International Maritime Organization, several other common satellite systems were created and joint U.S./U.S.S.R. space ventures organized.

VII. New world conferences were convened: on soil erosion, on mountain areas, on the world's cold zones and on the family. Repeat world conferences to review achievements became a common practice.

VIII. A World Institute for the study of national, regional and world management was established.

IX. Several new world agencies were created: a UN outer space agency; a world organization for the handicapped; a world organization of national parks; the International Bureau of Informatics in Rome and the International Standardization Organization in Geneva became specialized agencies of the UN; a United Nations International Fund for the Elderly (UNIFELD) was created on the pattern of

UNICEF; a world office for the study of war and accident prevention was created by the UN; the UN Institute for Training and Research (UNITAR) was transformed into a World Academy, and UN statistical services became a World Statistical Office.

X. Several countries had their delegates to the United Nations elected by popular votes.

XI. Several countries changed the name of their Ministry of Foreign Affairs to Ministry of World Affairs and Cooperation.

XII. A Commission on Subversion was created in the United Nations to which governments can submit complaints against foreign subversion.

XIII. A World Foundation was created to allow private citizens to contribute to world cooperation, humanitarian causes and peace through the United Nations and its specialized agencies and world programs.

XIV. The United Nations flag, emblem and hymn gained considerable ground as one-world symbols. The UN emblem was displayed on all international civilian aircraft to discourage terrorism and military interference.

XV. A World Court of Media Ethics was created to receive complaints against unethical treatment by the media.

XVI. Several nations replaced national holidays with world days, such as World Environment Day (5 June), International Day of Peace (third Tuesday in September), United Nations

Day (24 October) and Human Rights Day (10 December).

XVII. Multinational sovereign political arrangements such as the European Common Market, the European Assembly and the European Court of Human Rights were adopted in other regions.

XVIII. Several countries followed the example of the U.S. and Canada and created National Peace Academies. The University for Peace in Costa Rica developed a comprehensive peace strategy and training program concerned with every layer of our planet's reality (outer space, the atmosphere, the seas and oceans, the continents, down to the atom) and of the human condition (peace between nations, races, religions, sexes, generations, cultures, political systems, minorities, corporations, etc.).

XIX. More world ministerial councils were established along the pattern of the UN's World Food Council.

XX. A World Ethics Chamber was created to determine what was ethical from the world's and humanity's point of view rather than from that of nations, other subgroups and special interest groups.

XXI. The UN created a body for world ecumenism and religious cooperation to combat religious fanaticism and dogmatism.

XXII. As a result of renewed willingness of the big powers to cooperate internationally within the United Nations, the normal rule of decision-making became consensus rather than voting.

XXIII. A meeting of former Presidents of the General Assembly held during the fortieth anniversary year of the United Nations streamlined and energized the procedures and decision-making processes of the General Assembly.

XXIV. A minute of world silence for prayer or meditation together with the delegations to the General Assembly on its yearly opening on the third Tuesday of September (International Day of Peace) was widely implemented in the world. A World Association for the celebration of the International Day of Peace was created.

XXV. A World Core Curriculum was developed to serve as a common guide for global education in all schools of the earth.

XXVI. Following the creation of the United Nations University in Tokyo, the University for Peace in Costa Rica, the International Maritime University in Malmö and the International Institute for Training in Nuclear Physics in Trieste, several new world universities were created under the auspices of the United Nations and its specialized agencies for aviation, telecommunications, climatology, human rights, etc.

XXVII. A World Institute was created to study the head of state and government function, to foster cooperation and the exchange of experience between heads of states and government.

XXVIII. A World Peace Service was created, allowing young people to do world service in poor countries and with UN agencies instead of national military service.

XXIX. World standardization made considerable strides: e.g., the UN convention on road signals and traffic rules was applied world-wide; so was the World Health Organization's standard nomenclature of pharmaceutical products.

XXX. International consumer protection was promoted through worldwide cooperation of national consumer protection agencies.

XXXI. Strong revival of work on international taxation in order to combat international fiscal evasion. The U.S. formalized its proposal for the establishment of a UN World Bureau on Income Information.

XXXII. A World Court of Human Rights was established.

XXXIII. Commemorations of the anniversary of the UN were held every five years, keeping the 1985 anniversary motto: "United Nations for a Better World." During these anniversaries, not only the UN but all nations, institutions, religions, firms, associations and individuals asked themselves the questions: What have I done for a better world? What did I do wrong? What can I do better in the future?

Year 2000

12. Preceded by much public and governmental preparation and excitement, a Worldwide Celebration of the Bimillennium took place. Gratitude was expressed for having overcome one of the most dangerous periods of change on any planet in the universe. Innumerable, rich materials were published on the human journey and ascent over the last five thousand years and on hopes and remaining challenges for the future. The UN state of the world report 2000 highlighted the following accomplishments and failures:

  I. World population down to 5.5 billion people (against forecasts of 7.3 billion in 1970, during the twenty-fifth anniversary of the UN, and of 6.1 billion in 1985, during the fortieth anniversary); early child mortality reduced in nine tenths of the world; longevity progresses world-wide; racial and sexual equality achieved; UN world plan for the handicapped implemented; environmental deterioration halted, pendulum swinging back to improvement in many places; soil erosion, loss of tree cover and desertification considerably slowed down; industrialization, agriculture and economic conditions improve world-wide. The world's global warning systems work well. There is better coordination between global, national, local and individual policies and behavior. More accurate, truthful world information is available as well as better world education.

  II. No conflicts anywhere; all wars and disputes of the 1980s have been resolved; world security system is now in place; UN land, air and naval peace-keeping forces ready to intervene and guarantee the terri-

torial integrity of all nations; World Disarmament
Agency has begun to operate; reconversion of defense and arms industries has started; the military
are being used for constructive activities, helping
in natural disasters and being progressively transformed into police forces; the first nuclear weapons
were destroyed during the year amid public joy
and festivities; transfer of military expenditures to
efforts directed at greater world productivity and
help for the poor has become a priority issue. Plan
is to destroy armaments by 10 percent each year, in
order to achieve total disarmament of the planet by
2010.

III. Yearly state-of-the-world reports are now being
prepared by all UN agencies, as well as world programs on every global facet of our planetary home
and of the human condition. Plans and targets for
each next decade throughout the century will be
prepared and a general perspective 3000 issued in
2010.

IV. The UN has produced a new planetary ideology
and spirituality consisting of five basic harmonies to
be aimed at by humanity:

a. harmony between the human species and the planet
(population, conservation, environment, disarmament, etc.).

b. harmony of the human family and of its natural and
man-made groups (races, nations, cultures, languages,
religions, corporations, etc.).

c. harmony with the past and with the future (preservation of genetic material, of nature's elements, of the
earth's living species and flora, of cultures; preservation and preparation of a better and more beautiful
planet for future generations).

e. harmony with the heavens (religions have produced a code of divine or cosmic laws to be followed by all peoples and groups on our celestial body).

f. the fulfillment, happiness and harmony of the individual within the human family, the planetary home, the universe and the stream of time (the art of peaceful, happy, responsible, participatory living to be taught to all).

V. A Parliamentary Chamber has been added to the UN. Steps have been taken to introduce a new system of planetary management and governance: Harold Stassen's redraft of the UN Charter calling for an executive ministerial council, composed of ministers appointed by the different regions, to administer the two world commons (outer space and the seas and oceans) is being implemented. Strong worldwide revival of parliamentarianism.

VI. On the negative side: there are still 300 million malnourished on the planet and 600 million illiterates; poverty is still far from being eradicated world-wide; human rights are still often violated; urban growth remains unchecked in many places; mortality due to accidents, especially automobile accidents, and environmental diseases still rampant. Most nuclear armaments are still present on the planet. Atmospheric pollution is reaching the danger point.

2010

13. The first Decade of the New Planetary Age is now over. There are no conflicts and there were no nuclear accidents. The rate of arms destruction has encountered resistance and had to be slowed down to reach total disarmament in 2050 instead of 2010. But the trend is

expected to be more favorable as it becomes clear that the world is better off after each phase of arms destruction.

14. The state of the world reports show progress on most fronts. The world is now in an optimistic phase and as a result there is acceleration of human progress all round.

15. World management is improving everywhere. The UN World Climate Organization (formerly the World Meteorological Organization) has even devised specific plans and technologies to detect and to prevent the next ice age. We are becoming intelligent, knowledgeable masters of this planet, managing and taking good care of our cosmic globe.

16. Humanity is happier physically, mentally, morally and spiritually. More and more people are enjoying life in its rich, astonishing diversity and understand that life is a tremendous privilege. No other planet with life has as yet been detected in the universe. It is becoming increasingly evident that the cosmos has produced truly unique phenomena on this planet, especially human life with its constantly transcending consciousness and knowledge into the entire universe and stream of time, and responsibility therein. There is increasing recognition that we are a unique cosmic phenomenon as part of the evolution of the universe and that our duty is to help the cosmos succeed in its evolutionary experiment through the human species on this planet. The U.S. and the U.S.S.R. fully recognized their global and cosmic responsibilities.

17. The next phase of our evolution will therefore be a cosmic, divine age in which the earth will become a true showcase in the universe with human beings in

perfect physical, mental, moral and spiritual communion with God, the universe and evolution.

18. Conclusion: The charter drafted sixty-five years ago after World War II at the initiative of the United States proved to be one of the most remarkable documents of all times. From the moment the main impediment to the efficiency and good functioning of the UN, namely the cold war between the U.S. and the U.S.S.R., disappeared and all governments decided to implement the charter faithfully, the world entered a definitive era of peace and of orderly management of planet earth for the greatest happiness of all people admitted to the miracle of life.

AFTERWORD

The United Nations at Forty

Statement made on 31 May 1984 by United Nations Secretary-General Javier Pérez de Cuéllar to the opening meeting of the Preparatory Committee for the Fortieth Anniversary of the United Nations.

I welcome the decision of the General Assembly regarding the observance of the fortieth anniversary of the United Nations. Member States are aware of my views on the international situation and the challenges facing our Organization. I have expressed these in my reports of 1982 and 1983 on the work of the Organization. I am grateful for the care with which these views have been considered by a number of Member States and in the Security Council.

To me, the fortieth anniversary of the United Nations provides a further occasion not only to review the performance of the Organization over the past four decades but, above all, to encourage a rededication by Member States to the principles and purposes of the Charter, to promote interest in the work of the Organization and support for its efforts and to reinvigorate international co-operation in all fields of human endeavour. There can be little doubt that, if it is governed by such an approach, the observance can help further the cause of international understanding.

The General Assembly has wisely given us good time to think ahead and to prepare for the anniversary. It will be the special task of your Committee to make proposals to the thirty-ninth session of the General Assembly this fall. I assure you of my full co-operation and that of the Secretariat in the planning of the anniversary. At this opening of your first meeting, may I be permitted to share a few personal views with you.

First of all, I believe that nothing could be more valuable for the peace of the world than a firm recommitment by all Member States to their obligations under the Charter and its fundamental purposes. This recommitment needs to be expressed not so much through ceremony and in words as in policies and actions. A renewal of faith in the Organization is absolutely necessary to the future of the global community.

Second, I believe that it would be appropriate for every Member State to take a searching look at the impact of the United Nations and of its work on international life. This should include an objective assessment of the benefits, tangible and intangible, which have flowed to every Member State, as perceived in the perspective not of narrow short-term interests but of the entire human community and its evolution. It will also undoubtedly mean an examination of the weaknesses and shortcomings of the Organization and their cause or causes.

The aim should be to suggest what positive actions and improvements can be effected forthwith and during the last 15 years of this century until the bimillenium. I would like to see each Member State call upon its best thinkers and prominent citizens conversant with world affairs to undertake such a review and to propose concrete programmes of action in order to strengthen commitment to the aims and purposes of the Organization.

Third, the anniversary will provide a much-needed opportunity to give the people of the world a truthful account of what the United Nations can and cannot do, of its successes and failures, of its means and limitations, of its dreams and realities. During my travels in many countries, I am often struck by the low level of knowledge, prevalent among the people, about the United Nations at the very time when a much better awareness is so indispensable. May I express the hope that 1985 will witness the beginning of a serious educative effort to foster world-wide information about the United Nations and that Governments, the media and educators will play an important role in this endeavour.

Fourth, I am sure that future historians will consider the establishment and development of the United Nations system of specialized agencies and world programmes since 1945 as a most remarkable achievement of the international community during the second half of the twentieth century. What is involved in this process might well be the transformation of a community of nations into an international society, equipped with instrumentalities for the performance of essential global functions and the attainment of substantial benefits for all humanity, including its most-needed members, through the joint actions of Governments. The creation, development and work of this historically unprecedented international institutional system would merit to be brought to light during the fortieth anniversary.

Fifth, as the chief administrative officer of the Secretariat, one of the principal organs established by the Charter, I pledge once again my determination to administer, to guide and to seek to inspire the Secretariat so as to make it worthy of the confidence placed in it by Member States and by the peoples of the world. I will pursue my efforts to streamline Secretariat structures, to strengthen the efficiency of services rendered, to improve coordination and to eliminate duplication and waste.

Sixth, it seems to me right and proper that the world community should speak out frankly and with a full sense of responsibility towards the entire human family and its planetary home, about the shortcomings of Member States and of this Organization to fulfil such vital purposes as the consolidation of peace and security, disarmament, economic development and the promotion of human rights.

Last, but not least, may I express the fervent hope that every effort will be made to have the year 1985 stand out laudably as a year of peace, conflict resolution, restraint, international co-operation and friendship among nations. This would be the way of transforming an anniversary into a celebration.

Our preparatory work should lead, at the anniversary session of the General Assembly which might be attended at the highest possible level, to an objective and historical balance-sheet. We should count our successes as well as our failures. I refer here above all to the frightening course taken by the arms race, as well as to several protracted unresolved conflicts.

We need to work with determination on the negative items of that balance-sheet while drawing encouragement from the progress achieved. Animated by the will of all to make the journey of humanity on this planet less stormy, and happier than at present, we should work for the attainment of an era of peace and accomplishment that will give a new direction to the course of human destiny by the year 2000.

I leave out at this stage other personal thoughts relating in particular to the participation and role in the anniversary of other intergovernmental, non-governmental and regional organizations, of the media, of the academic world, of the churches, of international associations and business, of citizen's groups, of youth, of women, of prominent international personalities and thinkers, and of the international civil service. I might have occasion to refer to them during the preparatory process.

Already now, barely a day passes when I do not receive proposals, visits, ideas and expressions of support and help from many people and organizations interested in the anniversary. There seems to be so much despair and disillusionment in the world today that the United Nations appears to many as a last ray of hope and salvation.

As we embark upon our work, we may recall these lines written by Franklin Roosevelt on the last day of his life for a speech he intended to deliver at the San Francisco Conference:

> "The work, my friends, is peace: more than an end of this war—and end to the beginning of all wars. I ask you to keep up your faith. The only limit to our realization of tomorrow will be our doubts of today. Let us move forward with a strong and active faith."